Life is Positional Power & You Haven't Got It

Edmund Carpenter TWO ESSAYS

Persimmon Press · 2005

LIBRARY OF CONGRESS CATALOGING-IN-PUBLICATION DATA

Carpenter, Edmund Snow, 1922-
    Two essays / Edmund Carpenter.
        p. cm.
    Contents: Chief — Greed.
    ISBN-13:978-1-882903-13-9 (alk. paper)
    1. Heye, George G. (George Gustav), 1874-1957. 2. Indianists—United
States—Biography. 3. Museum of the American Indian, Heye Founda-
tion—History. 4. Indians of North America—Museums—New York
(State)—New York—History. I. Title

E56.C37 2005
973.04'9700747471—dc22   2005053512

ISBN 978-1882903-13-9

Persimmon Press
P.O. BOX 821
NORTH ANDOVER, MA 01845

This book contains two essays: *Chief*
                                   Greed
What links them is the Museum of the American Indian.
What differs is the tone.

Between chapters, I insert artifacts & ask:
What each meant to those for whom it was originally intended?
What motivated an 'outsider' to collect it?
What was its fate after Heye acquired it?

This disrupts continuity, but serves as a reminder that utilizing
& guarding this collection was the Trustees' primary duty.

I use the ampersand, but not when quoting.

GLOSSARY OF ABBREVIATES:

AMNH   American Museum of Natural History
ANS   Academy of Natural Sciences
APS   American Philosophical Society
BAE   Bureau of American Ethnology
BM   British Museum
CUMAA   Cambridge University Museum
HFL   Huntington Free Library
MAI   Museum of the American Indian
NMAI   National Museum of the American Indian
NYS-AG New York State Attorney General
UM   University Museum, University of Pennsylvania

CONTENTS

CHIEF

GREED

CHIEF

by Edmund Carpenter

with great indebtedness to Junius Bird

CHAPTER 1 George

George Heye (1874-1957)

Photograph courtesy National Museum of the American Indian, Smithsonian Institution

'. . . sardonic of eye and dead of pan,
even mocking of lip, but at no point hostile.
Only watchful. A big cigar smoked eternally
between his large fingers.'

Kevin Wallace

I met George Heye in 1940, but only briefly. However, I knew, often well, about a dozen who worked at his museum or collected for him in the field. None survive.

Fortunately, three recorded their impressions of him soon after he died. J. Alden Mason, Curator at the University Museum, Philadelphia, wrote the official biography.[1] E. K. Burnett, Heye's assistant & immediate successor, left an oral history.[2] Junius Bird, Curator at the American Museum of Natural History, spoke candidly in a *New Yorker* article by Kevin Wallace, 1960.[3]

Bird appears there under a pseudonym, but in quotation marks. He remains our best informant. Without him, the real George Heye would be forever lost. I quote Bird at length with the permission of his family.

'George always looked fresh up from the Wall Street of his father's day', said Junius Bird. 'A very downtown air. Just under six-four, weighing over 300 pounds, immaculately tailored in pale blue, with a big gold watch chain across his stomach and a big, canny mournful expression on his sagging flour bag of a face, centering around a big, sixty-five cent cigar. He smoked eighteen a day.

'A habit of power and of respecting only those with more power, or else those who stood up to him. The smell of leather chairs from his University and Lotus and Explorers clubs. The aura of Escoffier's and Oscar's cooking that he gorged himself on, training for it by breakfasting on a piece of dry toast and half a grapefruit and lunching not at all.'[4]

At the evening meal, commencing about 8:30 & continuing leisurely for at least two hours, Heye consumed such quantities of food, guests sat in bewilderment. 'Ah, the interesting canapés I remember eating', said Bird, 'surrounded by all that ugly Chippendale in the Heyes' apartment — a French robin named Autiel, hard-boiled plovers' eggs, venison liver, quarts of un-dyed black caviar with hot butter'.[5]

Heye never abandoned this Edwardian approach to gracious dining. His formal dinners, especially New Year's Eve, challenged staff & guests alike. He personally knew some of the great epicurean chefs on either side of the Atlantic & compiled recipes from them which he gave to cronies. Few found them practical: 'Take three cleaned, dressed suckling pigs . . .' or '. . . add four pounds of melted butter. . . .' In his own right, he was a cook of no mean ability. Well-known restaurants used some of his recipes.

'George', continued Bird, 'made perfect sense as the first-nighter paying a hundred bucks to have his car first at the curb after the show; and as the Santa Claus whose Christmas remembrances to the Riverside Drive traffic cops suspended all laws in his driving to work and back; and as the sentimentalist who hired Lauritz Melchior to render 'Auld Lang Syne' at the pagan routs he staged every New Year's Eve in the Waldorf's Cirque Room.

Where his protective coloration failed was with us. He stood out, *there*.'[6] *There* was

American Indian studies. Heye entered the field as a hobbyist. But two things set him apart from arrowhead collectors: a fortune & a monomania that still defies explanation.

EARLY LIFE

The fortune is easily explained. Carl Gustav Friederich Heye, George's father, owned a refinery & pipeline at Oil City, Pennsylvania. In 1876, he sold out to John D. Rockefeller for $50,000, taking $35,000 in cash, 150 shares of stock & a position that developed into head of Standard Oil's overseas shipping. George was his only son.

Carl Heye came to America as a young man & retained a great fondness for his native Germany. At 35, he married an American, Marie Lawrence, 24. They had two children, a daughter & George, called 'Baby George' by his nurse & mother until his late teens. He was said to worship both. Even in an age of Edwardian manners & class, his pampered childhood drew comments. One special event led to his picture in the *Times*. On his way to school, a few blocks away, on the morning of the great blizzard of 1888, he had to be pulled out of a snow drift by passing workmen.

George's playmates belonged to old Murray Hill families. New wealth & West European immigrants now mixed with the society of Edith Wharton. George grew up in the New York of *Father Knows Best*, whose author, Clarence Day, was his contemporary & lived around the corner.

Carl Heye's work took him to Europe at least once a year. The family accompanied him. From the time he was six or seven, George knew European cities. In all, he crossed the Atlantic, round-trip, 53 times, spending a total of nearly two years on luxury liners.

His father collected clocks, many of which he kept at his new home, 11 East 48th Street. All were synchronized to the split-second. This produced a bedlam of multitonal chimes each quarter hour, day & night. When his father died in 1899, George replaced the clocks with Indian pots. He later banned clocks from museum areas where he worked.

At 16, he enlisted in the Seventh Regiment, New York National Guard. The Seventh got called out once, to preserve order during a trolley strike. George served six years & remained a member of its veterans' association until his death.

SCHOOLING

In 1892, he entered Columbia University's School of Mines, located a few blocks from his home, where he continued to live. At school, he joined the S.O.B. Club, a floating game of Hearts. Several members later achieved prominence. One of them, Harrison Kerr Bird (addressed later as 'General' for his service as military secretary to a New York governor) recalled how he & George served as laboratory assistants to Professor Michael I. Pupin. Pupin perfected telephony by means of induction coils & contributed to the use of Roentgen rays. 'He liked us', said Harrison Bird, 'because we weren't irritatingly bright and we took him over to Schaefer's Brewery after lab . . . he couldn't have selected us on any basis of scholastic attainment.'[7]

'George', said the General, 'was the last boy in our neighborhood I would have suspected of getting a hobby on Indians, or on anything. [He] was the pleasant, unassuming, plump product of the well-regulated German background dominated by his father. [He] never spoke of any fondness for his father, though he mentioned admiring his administrative capacities. It certainly surprised me later to hear that George worked up enough administrative capacities to get himself a museum. I still mean to get up to take a look at his museum one day.

'Whenever we met in later years, we always matched for five dollars. I forget why, if I ever knew, but it was a fine and enduring friendship.'[8]

Another classmate, Paul MacGahan, recalled how, on preparing a joint graduation thesis, 'George persuaded me to go in with him on a study of the lubricating values of different oils . . . we found peanut oil of no value, but castor oil very fine for lubricating machines that operate at high temperatures. We also studied the effect of lubricating the inside of a growler — a covered can of beer — so as to get more beer and less foam when we sent freshmen to the brewery, across the open New York Central tracks, for a dime's worth of beer. There was also something about banana oil. . . . Professor Crocker was nonplussed when he read our thesis and would have flunked us, but didn't, on account of the Heye family's well-known oil background. For me, the engineering degree was a necessity. As to George, I hardly think he was seriously inclined.'[9]

ARIZONA, 1897

At 21, Heye received the degree of Electrical Engineer. For the next eight years, he undertook assignments for the White-Crosby Company: 'In 1897 I was sent to Kingman, Arizona, as assistant superintendent of construction for a branch track to a mine about seventeen miles distant. I obtained a number of Navajo Indians for use as laborers for grading the right of way.

'I lived in a tent on the work and in the evenings used to wander about the Indians' quarters. One night I noticed the wife of one of my Indian foremen biting on what seemed to be a piece of skin. Upon inquiry I found she was chewing the seams of her husband's deerskin shirt in order to kill the lice. I bought the shirt [it survives] . . . It was the start of my collection. Naturally when I had a shirt, I wanted a rattle and moccasins.'[10]

Naturally oversimplifies how one lousy shirt led to nearly 700,000 Indian specimens.

This was George's first time away from his mother, Marie Antoinette Heye. Tenting, desert air, camaraderie, delighted him. In later life, he went on 15 digs. He spent his second honeymoon on one, his bride in overalls. Both loved it.

He shipped his Indian things home. Back in New York, ten months later, he found 'quite an accumulation of Indian curiosa in his old room.'

But the collecting bug lay dormant, at least briefly. George tried to conform. He helped found a bank (Battles, Heye & Harrison) with offices in Philadelphia & New York. He supervised construction of a bridge across the Delaware River near Trenton; a trolley line in Pennsylvania; the Hudson Theatre on West 44th Street. The Hudson survives. Robert Edson played Richard Harding Davis' *Strongheart* there during Heye's management of the theatre. George enjoyed theatre company. He also joined clubs; learned about wines; bought Rolls-Royce (plural).

At thirty, he married Blanche Agnes Williams of Wellesley Hills, Massachusetts. They established domiciles at 677 Madison Avenue & at Roslyn, Long Island. From this came two children, Mildred & Lawrence. George's mother sent his Indian collection to add challenge to her new daughter-in-law's housekeeping.

COLLECTING

Up to this point, George confined his purchases to single pieces, chosen randomly. He liked to stroll over to F. V. Covert's Indian Store on Fifth Avenue, select whatever attracted him, then invited a curator over to tell him what he had. Covert's was mostly souvenirs, but had serious pieces as well.

A club acquaintance, Joseph Keppler, advised him that his Navaho pieces possessed more than amusement value. Keppler, an artist & *Puck* magazine executive, collected Iroquois masks. In 1912, he sold Heye some of these masks for $3000 & later the remainder for $12,000. Over the years, Heye added more Iroquois masks until he had over 750, by far the largest collection anywhere.

Keppler introduced him to Dr. Marshall Saville, an archeologist at Columbia. Saville, in Bird's words, 'saw in George valuable magpie tendencies, and decided they should be nurtured and guided.' With George Pepper, an archeologist at the American Museum of Natural History (AMNH), the two decided this opportunity called for something more than shopping at Covert's.

With their guidance, Heye bought several hundred Tularosa pots from New Mexico, then several hundred more from San Juan, Arizona. The next year, 1904, his mother financed a major dig in Mexico, still another in Puerto Rico. In 1906, Saville went to Ecuador. Excavations at Manabi proved to be one of the most productive digs ever undertaken in South America. Marie Heye financed all of it, as well as a two-volume report.[11] She also picked up the tab for nearly every museum expense, including George's purchases.

That same year, at Pepper's suggestion, Heye bought a major collection of Southeastern Indian objects, assembled by Joseph Jones of New Orleans. Jones' catalog, with brief entries, filled over 800 pages.

So it went. Until his wife objected, he kept everything at home. Then, in 1906, he rented a large room at Fifth & 39th Street. It soon proved inadequate. He took the second floor loft at 10 East 33rd Street, then added the third floor. This address became known as 'The Heye Museum', not because it welcomed visitors (appointment only), but because there was nothing else to call it.

Early in his collecting, Heye asked if he might avail himself of fumigation facilities at the AMNH. The request was denied on the basis of a prior ruling. This puzzled Heye. He'd funded their conferences, publications. What was the problem? George Pepper assured him it wasn't he who had objected.[12]

FRANZ BOAS (1858–1942)

The objection came from Franz Boas. Boas joined the staff of the AMNH in 1896, as a junior ethnologist. His writings soon established him as America's leading anthropologist. Nine years later, he moved to Columbia University. Under his stern guidance, anthropology became a discipline, with Columbia its world center.

On one occasion, five teenagers (Mark Harrington, Arthur Parker, Edward Sapir, Alanson Skinner, Frank Speck, all destined to become leading ethnologists) waited outside Boas' office. They knew each other from Covert's Indian Store. Boas emerged. They told him they wanted to study Indians. 'No, no', he said as he hurried away, 'you must yourselves study.'

I mention this to put in perspective Boas' professionalism. He deplored Heye's dilettantism, his entire *modus operandi*. None the less, the AMNH became involved with him. It stored part of his collection, expecting it to be donated. It also exchanged specimens with him.

Museums, like department stores, wanted one of everything under one roof. What they lacked, they traded to get. Heye did well in those trades, too well some felt. Moreover, when he moved his collection to Philadelphia in 1908, he took along more than he owned. He also took along George Pepper, Mark Harrington & Alanson Skinner, all AMNH staff.[13]

PHILADELPHIA

Heye already had Philadelphia connections. His former bank partner, Brattles, was a trustee of the University (of Pennsylvania) Museum. Heye had just advanced $2000 to buy a third of the specimens its Director, George Gordon, hoped to gather in Alaska.

If 'Colonel' Gordon had collected railroads, he might have linked oceans. Instead, he collected ancient art. He expected Heye to finance an American Indian collection & donate it.

About a dozen new staff were hired. Heye paid their salaries, in whole or in part. All were young. Most were exceptionally qualified. Few other jobs existed.

The only comparable undertaking was at the American Museum of Natural History. Morris Jesup, its President, funded the Jesup Expeditions. Franz Boas directed a remarkable team. They documented tribes on either side of Bering Strait.

Heye's collecting was less modest. He collected from both American continents.[14] Behind this lay no impulse to preserve. That impulse, the poet Larkin said, lies at the bottom of all art. No, no. Heye had something else in mind. He wanted to amass the greatest collection, *ever*.

Back from a dig in Panama, 1912, he found his wife had locked him out. She filed for divorce from the Roslyn address, alleging undue friendliness with an unnamed actress. She asked for the largest alimony sought up to that time in Kings County. The judge told a *Times* reporter: 'These New York society women make me tired. They go to fashionable hotels and drink highballs and smoke cigarettes instead of staying home trying to make their husbands happy. They ride up Fifth Avenue in their fine automobiles, with poodle dogs in their laps, and when they are married to a poor man, unfortunate enough to have a million dollars, they come into court and say that their "social position" requires an exorbitant amount of money. [Mrs. Heye] had a soft thing and she lost him. She will never get $78,000 from me.'[15]

He awarded her $15,000 a year. Heye may have resented the judge's comments about 'a soft thing.' But, more likely, he enjoyed his new freedom. He resigned all remaining business & engineering connections. 'I just thought "Wall Street doesn't owe me anything", so I quit.' He put his inheritance into public utilities, hired more archeologists & joined a crew digging an Indian cemetery in New Jersey.

The site overlooked the Delaware River. All went well until a local politician charged grave-robbing 'for mere wantonness.' The court fined Heye $100 & each of his crew $10. He appealed. The Supreme Court of New Jersey held that, though he might have 'violated the laws of decency and morality', he hadn't done so out of 'mere wantonness.' Judgment reversed.[16]

According to one observer, this experience gave Heye a sense of being needed. If so, that sense surfaced rarely. It never extended to his children who, motherless after 1924, lived in boarding schools & summer camps. Nor, ultimately, did it extend to his staff. But, at that moment: blue skies!

1915

In 1915, Heye married Thea Page. All agreed: the marriage was immensely successful. They spent their honeymoon in Georgia, excavating the great Nacoochee Mound. Movies show him in shirt-sleeves, her in overalls & pith helmet. He finds a superb Indian treasure. She embraces him. The scene is totally convincing.

Nacoochee was a major dig, jointly sponsored by Heye & the Bureau of American Ethnology. The BAE's Chief Curator, Frederick Hodge, supervised the work. Nacoochee disgorged quantities of what Heye loved most: spectacular art, including effigy vessels & a pipe of a raptorial bird whose open mouth served as a bowl.

At Nacoochee, a local boy, Charles Turbyfill, came aboard as waterboy. When the dig closed, Heye invited him to join his staff. 'I told my Daddy: "Mr. Heye wants me to go with him." He asked me if that's what I wanted. I said, "Yes."' Heye sent him off to join Alanson Skinner & Mark Harrington, then digging in Arkansas.

Others recognized Turbyfill's potential. Samuel Lothrop worked beside him on several digs. When Lothrop later went to Harvard, he urged Turbyfill to join him there & get a degree. 'But I told him, "Sam, you know I can't leave Heye."' He never did.[17]

Heye had up to six parties in the field at a time, organized by 'Colonel' Gordon. Archeologists saved endangered specimens. Ethnologists preserved timely information. The standard method for funding fieldwork then was to ask museums for advances on specimens to be collected. Heye was a regular backer. Shipments poured in. A few went to Philadelphia. Most went to New York.

Marie Heye died in 1915. At this point, Archer Huntington, adopted son of Collis P. Huntington, railroad magnate, offered land for a museum on Upper Broadway. Huntington planned a cultural cluster there, the Lincoln Center of its day. Heye accepted.

Gordon was devastated. Heye's collection was the centerpiece of Gordon's American displays, the keystone around which he'd built their joint holdings. He reminded

Heye of their 'unwritten understanding' about the ultimate disposition of that collection. He asked for compensation.[18]

EXCHANGE REQUIRED

Heye agreed, but said an exchange was required. His collection, he wrote, now belonged to the Museum of the American Indian. He said he was in no position to give away anything. However, the exchange need be only a token one, with the University Museum giving 'a few things of little value.'

Those 'few things of little value' turned out to be many things of great value. Consulting no one, Heye added them to his own collection & shipped the whole to New York. Then he stalled. Finally, as a 'slight token' of appreciation, he sent Gordon 'the larger and more bulky specimens' from a collection of junk. The first shipment infuriated Gordon. After two more shipments, he protested: 'In every instance the Museum already preserves better specimens. These donations . . . do not . . . add anything of value to our collections. . . . To one as familiar as yourself with Museum requirements and methods, my meaning will be quite clear without any further explanation.'[19]

Where did Heye, a canny buyer, ever get this stuff? 'As with all dedicated collectors, observed his assistant, E.K. Burnett, 'George was ruthless in his dealings. Oh, he was "done" every here and there, but the scale was greatly tipped on the side of doing unto, rather than done unto.'[20]

In this case, he got done unto. The collection surfaced in the Ferry Museum, Tacoma. Stewart Culin, collecting for the University Museum, stopped by in 1900. On the first floor he found 'a jumble of old newspapers, books, historical records, glass, pottery, arms and old clothes', plus an execution scaffold, 'in working order', used twice recently on the premises.

'The labels, such as they are, are misspelled and full of errors. Ariadne appears as "Aridna"; a pair of Chinese curtain hooks are marked "African headdress"; a wooden stamp for the sacred loaf of the Greek Church is stated to be a "Greek butter print" . . . a marble replica of the "Dying Gall."'[21]

Returning in 1905, Culin found the ground floor unchanged. Upstairs, however, was a Northwest Coast Indian collection offered for sale by Captain D. F. Tozier, U.S. Customs Service. According to Culin, 'His position, cruising constantly among Indian villages, gave him an opportunity to secure things which, according to common report, he frequently stole, or secured at nominal sums by the exercise of a show of force or authority . . . a thoroughly dishonest man.'[22]

Tozier asked $100,000. Stewart Culin, C. F. Newcombe & George Dorsey, all eminently qualified, examined the collection, piece by piece. Nothing interested them save 'seven large Kwakiutl house posts, old, black with age, admirably carved and highly interesting in design.'[23] The rest was crude; much of it covered with boat paint, with nothing labeled. Tozier couldn't recall where anything came from. No other buyer appeared. The price hit bottom. Heye bought the lot unseen.

When it arrived, he kept the house posts & dumped much of the rest on Gordon. Gordon shipped some of it to the Reading Public Museum (where it remains) & relegated the rest to a sub-basement. When the Schuylkill River rose, that basement flooded, 'greatly improving' the collection, in the words of one curator.

AUDUBON TERRACE

Philadelphia hosted a dinner in Heye's honor. He toasted his former associates, offered 'best wishes' & departed. His move to Audubon Terrace re-united his collection, since most of it never left New York. Archer Huntington's land holdings included scattered plots in what had been, until recently, a semi-rural area north of the City. Three of these lots ultimately went to Heye's museum.

This was the first. It was once part of John Audubon's farm, he of *Birds of America*. Later the Boltons, Grinnells & other aristocrats had summer homes there. The area declined. Huntington sought to salvage it by offering land, money & architectural plans (neo-classical) to cultural institutions willing to locate facilities there. Six agreed, including Heye's Museum of the American Indian (MAI), newly founded for this occasion. Huntington put $14m into Audubon Terrace.

Heye donated his collection, then numbering about 400,000 pieces. With it he gave a dollar per specimen to be paid in annual installments of $20,000. Before donating anything, he appointed himself 'Director for Life' & stipulated that only he could name its trustees. He also extracted, in advance, from trustees he appointed, an undated letter of resignation which, on at least one occasion, he exercised.

BOAS AGAIN

Rumors of Heye's plan reached Boas. A public museum, run according to the whims of George Heye, within walking distance of Columbia & a few subway stops from the AMNH, didn't sit well with Boas. He wrote twice, saying that science, education & the city would best be served 'by uniting your efforts with those of the American Museum of Natural History.'

He said he feared that, if Heye proceeded with his museum, he would be subject to adverse criticism & derive little pleasure from his public generosity. He mentioned the Duke of Loubat, a patron of archeology who 'always insisted in having things done in his own way.' Loubat, he said, became 'so disgusted with criticisms that he departed New York and turned to other fields.'[24]

Heye immediately replied: '. . . rather than go into a long and useless discussion, I will fall back on the sentence in your letter which I hereby quote: "It is obvious that nobody can deny that you have the right to do with your money as you please" . . . therefore, as far as I am concerned, the discussion is ended.'[25]

Boas & many of his students were Jews, but Heye was no anti-Semite. Some of his staff were, but that came with the times. Several viewed Indians as Vanishing Nobles & saw themselves as equally endangered. But not Heye. Harmon Hendricks, a trustee & backer, was Jewish. The problem lay elsewhere. Boas sought to shape anthropology into a scientific discipline. George Heye was no convert.

Boas didn't help. Charm wasn't his forte. I recall Frank Speck saying to me, 'I was one of Boas' first students. I dedicated two books to him. I helped him get relatives out of Germany. He never called me "Frank."'

Boas & Heye collided repeatedly. Boas thought poorly of Saville, then the Loubat Professor of American Archeology at Columbia University. Heye backed him. Boas helped establish an international school of archeology in Mexico & briefly served as director. He recommended J. Alden Mason for archeological work there. Mason, during the First War, got caught spying for the U.S.

Archeology & spying 'went with the territory.' At least three others (Samuel Lothrop, Sylvanus Morley, Herbert Spinden) were implicated, but elsewhere. Boas publicly withdrew his recommendation of Mason. Heye backed him. Correspondence between Boas & Heye makes awkward reading.

Shortly after the MAI opened to the public, Boas made a second effort. Nicolas Murray Butler, President of Columbia, met with Heye to discuss the question of amalgamation with Columbia. Heye remarked afterward: 'I am Director for Life by the articles of incorporation. Why should I make someone else my boss?'

Even if Heye had liked Boas personally, which he didn't, I doubt that anything would have dissuaded him from creating his own museum. Boas called this 'a matter of public interest.' Heye saw nothing 'public' about it. The public could visit his museum. Tax laws required it. But he never encouraged them. A bronze plaque read:

> HOURS: WEEKDAYS 2 TO 5 P.M.
> CLOSED SUNDAYS AND HOLIDAYS
> CLOSED DURING JULY AND AUGUST

23

Visitors encountered three small, dimly-lit floors. High Victorian cases served as little more than storage. Drawers below remained locked. Exhibits never changed. The bulk of the collection lay in the Bronx, five miles away, inaccessible to Indians, public & scholars alike. 'George didn't go out of his way to be a snob', said Junius Bird. 'He didn't have to.

'He saw no reason why he or the public should meddle in one another's preoccupations. Having bypassed tedious academic preparation for his collecting hobby, or mania, he wasn't too keen on scholars poking through his treasures. He expressed no need to explain himself, and didn't.'[26]

In his obituary of Heye, Samuel Lothrop said his 'museum is his monument.' Bird called that misleading. Heye, he said, had no monument in mind, certainly not one 'to make him a spectacle for unwashed crowds of future generations. . . . I doubt that [his] goal was anything more than having the biggest damned hobby collection anywhere. If stamps had won him over, instead of Indians, he would have bought himself the post-master generalship.'[27]

'Heye simply enjoyed his museum. He reveled in heavy Teutonic practical jokes with "The Boys", who called him "The Chief."'[28] 'The Boys' published *Museum Mustard*, a bi-monthly newsletter, posted in the museum & sent to colleagues in the field. One regular column, *Heye Jinks*, recorded Heye's latest capers. Another, *Hodge Podge*, reported Hodge's. The text was mostly doggerel, with comic illustrations. News items featured cars, bachelor status, 'Ed's new boater.' Indians went unmentioned.

For all his informal veneer, anyone who scratched Heye drew East 48th Street blood. He remained faithful to the neat, obedient, sentimental gemütlich world of his parents. He ran his museum with, as he put it, 'the unbeatable combination of German efficiency and American can do.' An orderly streak in him wasn't to be crossed. Two members of the staff, Alanson Skinner & Mark Harrington, forgot to empty an ash tray. Heye flayed them. They quit.

Two days later, both received this letter: 'I am hereby returning your self-respect by mail. I doubt that there will ever again be an incident as took place in your office yesterday. I am looking forward to seeing you both back on the job the day after you receive this.'[29] Years later, after Harrington had moved to another position, he named one of his sons John Heye Harrington.

Once a year, on a Saturday night, the staff returned for an all-night spoof-session enlivened by a midnight banquet catered by the Waldorf-Astoria. 'The meal began with a fish this long', one participant recalled, gesturing widely, 'and it built up from there. At the end, we pitched into eating up a great big molded ice cream Indian.'[30]

These were the good years. Anthropology then offered few salaried positions &
even less research funding. Heye's museum offered both. The staff didn't need to teach
or deliver babies or sell insurance. They were paid to do what they loved most: ex-
plore, dig, publish. A dream!

For Frederick Hodge it was Heaven. At long last, he could dig Hawiku, one of the
fabled Cities of Cibola, in Arizona. It was stormed by Coronado, 1540. Hodge first
saw it in 1886, as an assistant to Frank Cushing, known popularly as 'the man who
lived as a Zuni.'[31]

Between 1917-1923, with 6 Heye archeologists & 39 Zuni, Hodge systematically
explored this Arizona ruin. He uncovered over 1000 graves; 1200 pottery vessels; etc.
Movies show digging, pranks, camaraderie. A Heye trustee, Harmon Hendricks, funded everything.

CATALOGING

Heye handled cataloging. In bold, neat letters, he placed a number on every specimen. Surely no other museum director ever knew his collection so well, nor identified
with it so possessively. His penmanship was clear. He remembered details. He might
come upon a piece in storage, one he hadn't seen in years, then recount its origin,
probably in greater detail than he had recorded, for his records were minimal. Clearly
he enjoyed cataloging. A film shows him in shirt-sleeves, happily numbering a *kachina*
doll, cigar ashes everywhere.

Years later, talking among themselves about events all had witnessed, several staff
recalled 'The Chief' with affection & wonder. To them, he was Trickster, that mythic
figure who cheats the winner of his prize & the Devil of his due. They felt privileged to
have known him. Others felt otherwise. To them, Heye ran his museum out of a back-
room, like a Yoknapawpha sheriff. True, he hired scholars, but soon replaced them
with non-scholars, who delighted in his capers.

WHY INDIANS?

Why not? Heye wanted a good time. An Indian hobby allowed that: collect, travel,
camp, all in Edwardian style. He answered to no one.

The official explanation is that Heye devoted his life & fortune to saving a vanishing
legacy. That's a stretch. True, most thought Indian culture doomed. Few tried to stop it.
Fewer still sought to preserve anything. Even among those who noticed, motives varied.
Some recognized the human value of that legacy. For others, preservation was expiatory:

Having wiped out or subjugated all peoples who had not had the advantages of a Christian training in gentleness, humility, and other-worldliness, the Puritan Palefaces of America and Europe were very contrite and tried to make up for it to those who were left behind.

Wyndham Lewis, *Palefaces*

Bird thought this theory utterly missed George Heye. 'George had no sense of sin. He didn't give a hang about Indians individually and he never seemed to have heard about their continuing problems in society. The only Indian he ever hired was a driver and interpreter named Amos Oneroad, who didn't last. George didn't buy his scientific materials as a means of studying the life of a people, because it never crossed his mind that that's what they were. He bought them as commodities — for what, he didn't say. He was neither the student wooing 'truth' nor the social climber wooing 'prestige', like Rothschild with his birds and Henry Huntington with his books and Queen Anne with the clothes she bought off [a visiting Mohawk's] back, sending him back home in smart London tailoring.

'George didn't collect [to enhance] his standing around his clubs, where he rarely let on he had a museum. His motives weren't any of the usual ones. Not school spirit. Nicolas Murray Butler wanted the collection for Columbia . . . but George saw no reason to let the hobby get out of his control. It wasn't to endow a great civic institution: he turned down the American Museum of Natural History's bid for his stuff on the same grounds.'

According to Bird, 'It wasn't even simple boyish acquisitiveness, like Hearst's. George was fortified by sufficient monomania to build up a disciplined, superlative collection in just one category, whereas Hearst ran wild though 504 categories — 505 if you count newspapers — and wound up with everything, signifying nothing, from Richelieu's bed and a crated Spanish monastery to the superb [Plains & Pueblo shields] that George got, after Hearst's tax accountants instructed him to unload his jumble at Gimbel's.

'You could dig up [some explanation] and mangle George's biography to fit into it, but I prefer to explain George as a difficult fellow determined to have a good time. He was eighty the last time I saw him, in a night club not far from here, with a blonde at each elbow and champagne in front of him, presenting a cheerful sight that was neither undignified nor unattractive. He was maddening, but he won my grudging admiration.'[32]

Shrunken Men

No exhibit proved more popular than Heye's two shrunken men. Children raced to see them. Postcards outsold all others. Surrealist artists, refugees in New York during the Second War, invited friends to see them. Neighborhood children provided an explanation. One figure, they said, was a former missionary, the other his native assistant. Both had been hexed by a local witch doctor.

The smaller of the two, a mulatto, 26" high, appeared in an 1898 exposition in Guayaquil, Ecuador. Marshall Saville, one of Heye's archeologists, heard about it, tried to buy it, then lost track of it. In 1922, it resurfaced in New York. Heye bought it for $600. The seller, Juan Krateil, a Polish mining engineer, was President, Sociedad Anonima de Brea y Petroleo, Lima. He said he obtained the body from 'a Spaniard en route from Callao to Panama.'

Saville assigned this oddity to the Jivaro Indians of Tierra Oriente. Heye already owned 15 Jivaro shrunken heads.[1] However, an entire body was unknown.[2] Saville & Heye were delighted.

A photograph of this mummy, released to the press, received worldwide coverage. Among those who saw it was Dr. Gustave Struve, currently resident in Ecuador, but formerly of Lima. Struve immediately advised the museum that the mummy had been stolen from him in 1920. The thief, he said, had been convicted, but escaped with his booty.

The Secretary of the Heye Board wrote to the President, Banco Mercantil Americano del Peru, Lima, inquiring discreetly about Struve & Krateil.[3] He also hired a New York detective to check out Krateil, then resident in New York. The detective reported Krateil's business dealings with Henry L. Doherty; his association with one Cavallo (wanted in Peru), his departure from New York for a world cruise aboard his private yacht, *Speejacks*, but nothing about the mummy.[4]

The Lima source replied that Dr. Gustave Struve was unknown locally, but not 'a notable medical doctor, nor a person well-known in society.'[5] His identity was soon solved. He arrived at the museum, bringing along a second mummy, 31" high. He identified it as a bearded, blond Spanish soldier. It bore some resemblance to Robert E. Lee. Dr. Struve also had a shrunken embryo. All three, he said, he acquired during six years' residence among the Jivaro. Heye settled Struve's claim on the mulatto ($500); purchased the soldier; inscribed 12/6201 on its back; then exhibited the two together.

SHRINKING HEADS

The Shuar (*Jivaro*, in Spanish, means 'savage') shrank & preserved enemy heads as trophies (*tsantsa*). They severed the head; slit it from neck to crown; then carefully peeled away the skin. Next, they closed the incision & boiled the skin, extracting the natural oils.

A vine, threaded around the base of the neck, helped restore the original shape. Eyelids were sewn shut, lips sealed with wooden pegs & the head half-filled with hot sand. It was then whirled by the hair to distribute the sand. As the sand cooled, it was replaced & the whirling repeated.

When the desired size was achieved, facial hair was singed off & the skin polished & blackened. This last step prevented the enemy soul, blinded by darkness, from escaping & causing mischief.

The method was simple, but demanding. It took days. Facial features required constant smoothing & molding with hot, flat stones. Finally a feast, honoring the 'lord of the head', completed this ritual.

The Lima correspondent had mentioned a 'young doctor [not Struve] who learned to dry heads in a manner analogous to that employed by the Jivaros.' That young doctor wasn't alone. Heads brought good money. Graves & morgues offered a limitless supply.

Even today, Jivaro shrunken heads enjoy an international market. Thousands enter that market each year. Nearly all are fakes. Monkey or sloth heads may be used, or fur may be mounted over a mold, then trimmed. These are easily detected: eyebrows grow in opposite directions or are 'brush cut.'

Heye soon learned to recognize fake heads. In the 1930s, he unloaded these on Seattle's Ye Olde Curiosity Shop, including a female with torso. Heye & the proprietor were 'staunch friends', but business was business.[6]

DR. GUSTAVE STRUVE

In 1993, an American journalist, Caroline Alexander, asked the director of a Guayaquil museum, Olaf Holm, 'Whodunit?' He said he'd heard it was medical students, as a joke. 'In those days, yellow fever was uncontrollable. Unclaimed bodies were stacked in the morgue.'

Ms. Alexander found a 'Jara Gustavo Struve' listed in the Quito telephone directory. She called. The man who answered identified himself as the 75-year-old son of Dr. Gustave Struve: 'He left us when I was three . . . a few postcards, toys, then nothing . . . an atmosphere of hate.'

Asked about the mummies, the son replied, 'Papa used to make the mummies.'[7]

CHAPTER 2　Museum

On several trips to Europe in the 1920s, Heye took one of his motor cars. He &
Thea toured. In particular, Scandinavia delighted them. So did sentimental trips to his
father's homeland. They stayed in romantic old inns.

On all these trips, he bought in quantity. Pre-Columbian art, taken to Europe in the
1870-80s, returned with him. In Paris, Charles Ratton & Eugene Goupil found treasures for him, including conquistadores' loot: gold objects not melted down.

In London, W. O. Oldman came up with early material, including Woodland,
Northwest Coast & Peruvian treasures. He also had a large number of incised clubs
from British Guinea. Though made in traditional manner, these were early souvenirs,
intended for European curio cabinets. One example came from a 17th century ship-
wreck. Souvenirs from Brazil dated as early as the 16th century.

Heye's purchases always traveled on the same ship with him. Cartons & crates
might fill a large moving van. He wouldn't leave the ship until every piece was cleared
& in the hands of his transfer agent.

In 1929, he received an honorary doctorate from the University of Hamburg. The
citation said, apparently without irony, that he ran his museum 'in a unique way, according to his own ideas and experience.' He remained inordinately proud of this title.

Thea Heye liked to be called Frau von Heye. She had two interests: her husband &
his museum. A legendary hostess, she kept her large apartment at 270 Park Avenue
'looking like a florist shop.'[1] There she entertained the Trustees after Board meetings
— graciously, lavishly. Each dinner was a fiesta. Segments of the Seventh Regiment
Band played.

FORD & HENDRICKS

Thea arranged for Heye to meet people who could support his museum. Two
Trustees were particularly helpful. James Bishop Ford (1844-1928), perennial Com-
modore of the Larchmont Yacht Club, was Vice President, U. S. Rubber. He gave the
museum, over the years, several million. Harmon Hendricks (1846-1928), an owner of
Hendricks Brothers Metalworks, gave less, but financed expeditions.

Both were bachelors & about the same age. Both had taste, wealth. Hendricks lived with his sisters in the same building with the Heyes. He'd been a friend of Heye's father.

Ford & Hendricks were devoted to Thea. They donated specimens to the museum in her name. Anything listed as 'Presented to the Museum by Mrs. Thea Heye' came, in fact, from them. Hendricks gave the William Penn Treaty wampum belts; Colombian gold treasures; much more. Ford gave Mexican turquoise mosaics; Caribbean & Meso-American treasures; Peruvian textiles; much more.

Two magnificent, 16th century Peruvian textiles, Colonial Period, appeared at auction in 1924, perhaps the first of their kind to be offered for sale in New York. The auction house (now Sotheby's), not knowing what they were, identified them simply as 'covers.' Saville knew. Ford bought both for $1100 & presented them to the Museum in Thea's name.

Ford also bought Colombian gold work through the Amsink Gold Company, New York. Amsink billed by the ounce, then added a premium. Their principal buyers were dentists. No consideration was given to artistic value. On one occasion, 8 specimens weighing 92 ounces cost Ford $1,226.93.

BOARD OF TRUSTEES

The MAI Board lacked the clout of the Met's Board, but several trustees had money or power or both. Willard V. King, friend & advisor to Pierpont Morgan, served for 27 years. During the financial panic of 1907, he acted as Morgan's confidential courier, relaying messages between Morgan's office & Wall Street.

Archer Huntington, adopted son of Collis Huntington, served 39 years. Minor C. Keith, *El Papa verde* (The Green Pope), built the banana empire of United Fruit Company. They cleared plantations in nine Central American countries. As a result, he amassed an extensive archeological collection, principally from Nicaragua & Costa Rica. Much of this went to the Museum.

Rudolph R. Haffenreffer, Jr., had breweries at Narragansett Pier (Narragansett Beer & Ale) & Boston (Pickwick Ale). Both breweries were famous. He also owned Herschoff Ship Yards, Bristol, Rhode Island, where many American ships were built to defend the International Cup.

Blair S. Williams, 'an old, old friend', served on the Heye Board, as did his son, Blair S. Williams II, then John S. Williams, Sr., & finally John S. Williams, Jr. All were investors at a family firm. The family established a Shaker museum at Chatham, New York. Their contributions to the MAI continued into the 1970s.

Frederick Kingsbury Curtis was the senior partner of Curtis, Mallet-Prevost & Colt, a famous Wall Street firm. He became a trustee at the founding. A partner, Mallet-Prevost, had an unusual background. During the Civil War, he rejected Appomattox & rode south to West Mexico. There he married into a wealthy Mexican family, established a ranch & sent his son to Harvard Law School. When the son joined Curtis, he was one of the few on Wall Street who spoke Spanish & knew Latin America. He's remembered for celebrated cases. One involved a false claim to much of New Mexico & Arizona. The claimant inserted fake documents in archives, awaiting their discovery. Mallet demonstrated the ink was recent.

BUDGET

'It was Mr. Heye's usual custom', said Burnett, 'about the middle of March to get the "boys" together in what he called a budget meeting. The fiscal year of the Museum ended on March 31 and he prepared for the following year by establishing a budget and suggesting to the gentlemen present that they might do what they could to make ready the funds to meet that budget. Sometimes these budgets, or so they would now seem, were just gathered hurriedly from Cloud Nine. But, be that as it may, the supporters upon whom George Heye depended never failed to meet his estimated requirements.'[2]

At the 1928 budget meeting, Ford scribbled '$85 JBF' on a slip of paper. Days later, he died. His executors rejected that slip as without legal status. The courts felt otherwise. The Museum received, with interest, $93,130.87.

Willard King proposed Albert Gallatin as a trustee. He was elected, but resigned after two Board meetings. According to Burnett, that second meeting must have been the March Budget meeting.

KING PHILIP MUSEUM

Rudolph Haffenreffer collected many things, including Indian objects. To this end, he founded, on his Rhode Island estate, the King Philip Museum. He was particularly interested in local material, especially artifacts from Burr's Hill, a 17th century Wampanoag Indian cemetery.

A local railroad owned Burr's Hill. They used it for sand. At the same time, they allowed Charles Read Carr to excavate there, specifying that all finds be deposited in the George Hail Free Library, Warren, Rhode Island.

In 1928, Haffenreffer hired Foster Saville, ex-MAI staffer & brother of Marshall

Saville. Beginning about 1918, Foster Saville assembled, for the MAI, 122 artifacts from Burr's Hill. He obtained these from Carr's widow & relic hunters. In 1934, Heye sold about half of his Burr's Hill material to Haffenreffer.[3]

Between 1931-1945, Haffenreffer bought various things from Heye for his King Philip Museum.[4] According to legend, they arranged chairs on opposite sides of a wide table. From each chair hung a feathered bonnet. They donned these, lit cigars, then Heye brought out, from under the table, one at a time, object after object.

THE EXPLORERS CLUB

James Ford preceded George Heye as President of the Explorers Club, a New York club of wealth, power, patriotism. Few explorers belonged, though surely someone paid the fees of Matthew Hensen, who accompanied Robert Peary to Greenland. Hensen, a forgotten Black man, lived in Harlem.

Members dined well in paneled rooms, listening to lectures of distant ordeals. Peary's efforts to plant the American flag, first in Greenland, then allegedly on the North Pole, received secret funding through the Explorers Club.

James Ford regularly supported the Explorers Club, American Geographical Society (AGS) & MAI. In his oral history of the Museum, Burnett believed Heye diverted Ford's geographical contributions to the MAI, but never explains how Heye might have done so.

THE ANNEX

During the First War, military cartographers occupied the AGS, as well as the newly completed MAI. The two buildings faced one another across Audubon Terrace. During construction, then military occupancy, Heye's collecting never paused. By the time he moved into the new building, it was far too small. By 1925, it was bursting.

To meet this problem, Huntington erected the Annex, a brick storage center in the Bronx. Completed in 1926, its entrance bore Indian motifs in limestone. Trustee Curtis contributed heavily to its construction. Huntington added $20,000 to fence its six acres. In this park-like setting, Heye erected four real totem poles, an authentic Seneca log cabin, plus tipis of poured concrete. A staff ethnobotanist, Melvin Gilmore, planted an Indian garden, financed by Thea Heye & cultivated by school children.[5]

New acquisitions arrived weekly. Soon vaults became so crowded, so jammed, one only entered sideways. Beads covered the floor. Water craft were stacked like cordwood next to a coal-burning furnace.

The Annex included a small apartment for a caretaker. Heye asked Turbyfill to serve as Keeper of the Collections. 'For eleven years you've been living like a jack rabbit, in Pullmans and rock shelters and houseboats and tents and hotels. You're due for some home life with your wife and kids. I've picked you to take charge of the Annex.'[6]

Years later, Turbyfill described that scene: 'anthropologists were all over the place, writing their scientific books, and writing short stories for magazines when they thought Heye wasn't looking. When five o'clock came, nobody wanted to go home. Heye used to drop in here and eat strawberries out of my wife's colander and try to warn me off the stock market and the Democratic Party. We agreed on being Giant fans, the only difference being that once he tried to buy the team.'[7]

When Turbyfill mentioned writers, he referred to A. Hyatt Verrill (1871-1954). At 17, as an art student at Yale, Verrill collected & photographed fauna in the Dominican Republic for Yale's Peabody Museum. Back home, he opened a photography studio specializing in natural history. He met Heye around 1905 & joined his staff.

Verrill wrote books on lost tribes, ancient cities, cannibals, mysteries, buccaneers, treasure hoards, strange creatures, cars, radios, sailboats. One year alone, he published seven. None are noteworthy:

'As my mind harks back to my jungle days, as I recall the risks I took, the hairbreadth escapes I had, the accidents I endured with Death hovering over me, I marvel that I survived.... [I] recently completed my 115th book.'[8]

Many were written on museum time. Heye, convinced he was being taken, dismissed him abruptly, 1926.

FREDERICK HODGE (1867-1935)

Before joining Heye, Hodge served as Chief Curator, Bureau of American Ethnology. There he edited the Bureau's *Annual Reports,* grand publications of high scholarship. Single volumes might exceed a thousand pages, large format, well illustrated, colored maps, available free by writing to your Congressman.

Hodge hoped to maintain that standard at the MAI. In 1918, Huntington endowed a publication fund for $125,000. Hodge immediately demanded scholarly reports from staff & field-collectors alike. From 1921 to 1923, the Museum published, or prepared for publication, 37 books & pamphlets, totaling 2,842 pages. Some were of exceptional quality. Formats varied. Heye insisted, over the objections of scholars & librarians, that two series be 26x40 cm., the size of field notebooks. He never explained.

In 1924, Hodge published *The Rappahannock Indians of Virginia* by Frank Speck. That same year, Virginia passed its Racial Integrity Act. This classified Virginia Indians as Colored, subjecting Indians to the discrimination Negroes suffered. It also required that they serve in Negro regiments. A single exception was made in the case of socially prominent Whites who claimed descent from Pocahantas.[9]

Dr. W. W. Plecker enforced this Act. He warned Speck & Heye that, as author & publisher of the Rappahannock book, they qualified for arrest in Virginia. 'In Charles City and New Kent counties, these Negroes in 1900 gave a big "fish fry" to their white friends, at which time they announced their desire to become Indians. Three lawyers, for fees . . . of $2.50 each . . . issued cards to them declaring that they were "Indians."'

'I am sure', Heye replied, '[that your resentment against the Heye Foundation isn't as great as that] felt by this organization toward the citizens of Virginia who, for political or other reasons, are trying to inform us as to what stand we should take toward the Indians of their State.' Heye never backed down.[10]

PHYSICAL ANTHROPOLOGY

Antebellum America was racist, top to bottom, North & South. This included scientists: Louis Agassiz, Samuel Haldeman, Samuel Morton. Morton's *Crania Americana*, 1839 (superbly printed & bound), rated Indians midway between Caucasians & Ethiopians. Until Boas challenged racism & phrenology, few doubted.

Heye, to his credit, wanted no part of this nonsense. From 1915 to 1928, Dr. Bruno Oetteking served as the MAI's Curator of Physical Anthropology. Born in Hamburg, 1871, he trained in anatomy & came to America to work at the AMNH, on skeletons excavated on the Jesup Expedition.

Heye established a lab near Audubon Terrace. Oetteking's assistant was Dr. James B. Clemens, Heye's brother-in-law. Oetteking & Clemens published reports on skeletons from Alaska, California & the Southwest Desert; deformed skulls; etc. Later, Oetteking joined the medical faculty of Columbia University, 1920-1938, serving the MAI part-time after 1920.

HUNTINGTON FREE LIBRARY (HFL)

According to Junius Bird, 'James Ford held a good opinion of books, which Heye didn't.' In 1926, Ford purchased Saville's library for $25,000, Hodge's for $15,000: over 20,000 volumes.

How could two academics assemble such libraries? Scientific institutions traded publications, by-passing currency exchange. Until about 1940, scientific & commercial publishing remained separate. In lieu of royalties, authors received enough copies to distribute among colleagues. Scholars with limited incomes often assembled professional libraries.

Ford added rare items: a *Molina Dictionary*, Spanish-Nahuatl, glossed in Matlatzinca, 1555; manuscript diary of Daniel Claus, 18th century Indian agent; Kingsborough's *Antiquities of Mexico* (9 vols.); early *Jesuit Relations* (52 vols.); the 1685 Eliot *Bible* (2nd ed.); Coblentz' *Maxmillian's Travels in the Interior of North America* (1st Ger. ed.); etc.

Collis Huntington came by this Bronx, 1882, red brick, High Victorian Gothic building by default. Its original donor willed funds to build it, but the community declined to maintain it. It stood vacant for ten years. Huntington, who had a summer home nearby, assumed this responsibility. Adding quarters for a librarian, he opened it to the public, 1894.

In 1930, Heye transferred the MAI library from the museum's basement to the HFL, a short walk from the Annex. Its paneled Reading Room has a balcony from which Scriptural lessons were once read on Sunday evenings. Over a working fireplace hangs a huge, somber portrait of Collis P. Huntington, railroad magnate.

To provide for the Indian books & to honor his father, Archer Huntington added a modern wing. He also endowed future purchases. The library continued to benefit from museum exchanges. Its Indian holdings reached 40,000 volumes. Heye appointed Dr. E.K. Burnett, a podiatrist, as librarian of the HFL. Burnett edited & published various manuscripts. He worshipped Thea & delighted in the Chief's antics. When Heye died, 1957, the Board made him the Director of the MAI until 1960, when he retired.

The very best intentions — and vast sums — went into the HFL. To date, it served few. In 2004, pursuant to a court order, it was transferred to Cornell University.

Sacred Mat

In the 17th & 18th centuries, collecting belonged to gentlemen. Cabinets of curiosities reflected wealth, leisure. They added to the owner's 'mystique', separating 'him from lesser men.'[1] Military men favored trophies. Dilettantes mixed art & curios. Serious collectors focused on natural history. No matter how small the village, how remote the colony, mail linked them to the world of science.

Samuel L. Mitchell (1764-1834), New York physician, collected.[2] Born on Long Island, he studied medicine in Edinburgh & law in New York. He served in the U.S. Congress & Senate, published a geography of North America, a catalog of New York fish, a guide to New York City & much more. He also founded & edited America's first medical journal (1797-1824). During all this, he collected.

Donations to the New York Lyceum of Natural History, which he helped found, 1817, exceeded 1400 specimens.[3] His house 'groaned with . . . rocks, fish, animal skins and scientific apparatus.'[4] His wife once threw out the putrid hide of an anteater. Boys retrieved it. Failing to recognize it, Mitchell re-bought it, or so the story goes.

Mitchell obtained this mat from Captain Richard Whiley, U.S. commandant, Fort Mackinac, 1799-1802. Whiley got the mat 'as an offering of friendship on the part of an aged and venerable chief from the remote regions of the Northwest.'

Whiley moved to New York, 1802. By 1816, the mat, along with a pouch, were in Mitchell's collection. We know this thanks to Charles Hamilton Smith (1776-1859), a British spy posted to America to evaluate U. S. military capabilities along the northern border. Smith posed as a naturalist. It was an easy cover, for he was a published author & gifted watercolorist. While in New York, he sketched the mat & pouch in Mitchell's collection.

Mitchell called the mat a gift of 'extraordinary value.' It is. It's a rare, rare document of immense historical interest. For one thing, it employed 'invisible sewing.' As Mitchell noted: 'The stitching is so nicely done that the skin is not punctured through in any single instance; the needle, as in skillful tailoring, only passing deep enough in the leather to secure the work.'[5]

'Invisible sewing' was used for waterproof garments, especially moccasins. Otherwise, the technique was reserved for the sacred. That it pre-dated metal needles we know from ancient examples preserved in dry caves. The technique is analogous to needle-and-thread tattooing where tattoos were stitched into the skin by drawing blackened sinew through the epidermis.

INTERPRETATIONS

Mitchell believed the robe depicted a village surrounded by dancers 'capable of partaking of adventures in the forest.' Smith saw it as a flat map depicting a palisade, circular houses, people & a central temple with two idols.[6]

I see it as a three-dimensional cosmic map rendered in two-dimensions. If I'm right, it belongs to the same genre as *Midewinwin* cult, birch bark scrolls of the Ojibwa. It also shares much with Asian *mandalas*, prayer carpets, magic mirrors & other cosmic diagrams. Many were designed to be viewed as three-dimensional. They make no sense as flat art.

A Siberian shaman stands on a bearskin mat (representing the World of Darkness) or on a deerskin mat (representing the World of Light). From there he departs to Other Worlds. Chinese tomb mirrors reflect this solar image, with the earth below & intervening clouds in each corner.

A common Asian form, representing the Upper World, shows a mountain, its central peak penetrating the Sky Dome. Diagrams of the Lower World reverse this symbolism.

In Woodland cosmogony, Twin Underwater Panthers guard this Lower World. Their presence alone identifies this mat as a guide & map of the World of Darkness, as conceived by the Ojibwa.

GROUND LEVEL

Start at ground level. An unbroken chain of human figures surrounds the whole. In this iconography, dead people, ancestors, generally appear headless. These have heads & presumably represent the living. Even today, among Woodland people, observers at a *seance,* join hands around a performing shaman, exactly as here.

Descending, we encounter a square enclosure with opposing design elements. In each corner appears a loop, possibly a feather. If so, it may represent four birds, one in each corner, sometimes seen on shamans' robes or mats.[7]

Within this square are eight *mandala*-like circles, each accompanied by one or two 'floating' figures, possibly ancestors. Every circle duplicates one opposite it. Four circles, one in each corner, have strap-like, exterior extensions. I offer no explanation. Others have birds in each center. Again, I'm ignorant. These details had meaning to those for whom they were originally intended. I'm not privy to their knowledge.

Next, we encounter two enclosures: the first, square; the second, round. I believe they represent additional levels of descent. At the bottom, we meet the Twin Guardians whose help the shaman seeks.

In 1925, Daniel Carter Beard donated this shaman's mat, plus an associated pouch, to MAI. Beard was a popular illustrator, as well as the first National Boy Scout Commissioner.

CHAPTER 3 Accessioning

'Once a year', Junius Bird said, 'George picked up some new limousine and made a pilgrimage at ninety miles an hour to California. He paused en route at every wayside hamlet, located the local mortician and weekly editor, and asked for word of people lately deceased, or likely to become so shortly, who might be leaving an Indian collection behind. Chauffeurs couldn't drive fast enough to suit him, so he made the poor devils cringe in the back seat until he pulled up for the night and turned the wheel over to them, telling them to gas and garage the car and have it waiting in the morning. Every few years Heye might stop at a signal long enough to fall into conversation with a chauffeur, realize his perceptiveness, and give him a field commission as an anthropologist.

'One curator, William Stiles, came over from the phone company to drive Heye around and do other jobs. One year, George lost his rapport with Rolls-Royce and Locomobiles, and switched to Pierce-Arrow. The Pierce-Arrow people sent him one of their products equipped with a kind of mechanic-in-residence, an ex-racing driver named Ed Coffin, who shortly developed into one of the best archeological photographers anywhere and was running digs for George.'[1]

Edwin F. Coffin remained on staff until 1932. Through his efforts, the Museum acquired a large number of prints dating back to the last century. He personally photographed digs. He also filmed various tribal activities. Only the Smithsonian had a better collection. In 1989, the Smithsonian took over the Heye collection. It now has both.

IRRESISTIBLE BARGAINS

On these annual trips to the West Coast, though Heye took a chauffeur, he preferred to drive every mile himself, sometimes immense distances in a day, a remarkable feat considering roads & laws. After 1942, he crossed the continent by train, hiring a car in Los Angeles. These were buying trips.

Before setting out, he'd tell his assistant, Ken Burnett, 'Don't expect any shipments — no money this year — just going out to see old friends.' Knowing Heye, Burnett increased shipping funds & cleared space.

Soon brief messages alerted the staff to the imminent arrival of 'a few things.'

Crates, cartons, barrels arrived. The overflow went to the basement. Twitted about this on his return, Heye puffed contentedly on a cigar: 'irresistible bargains.' He promised to cover for his profligacy by giving up lunch — something he never ate.

One summer, Heye drove through the Canadian Rockies. North of Banff, he passed an encampment of Slavey Indians who had moved down from the tundra to take advantage of the tourist trade. Heye drove over one day and found an aged lady living in a skin tipi. She had a number of rather good Indian specimens. These he purchased, one at a time, including even some of her cooking pots. Then he asked her if she wouldn't like to sell the tipi. She agreed. He gave her $30 extra. 'Now', she said, 'me very happy. Now all me got is money.'[2]

EARL HORTER

Heye skipped the relic route. He ignored junk shops, flea markets, yard sales. He knew where the best pieces were: in existing collections. He had agents, everywhere. An estate auction in rural Ontario, 1927, included two Indian items. The Royal Ontario Museum submitted a low bid. They hoped no one else knew. Heye did. He won.

Before important auctions in the East, his representative met with local curators (Spinden, BM; Wissler, AMNH; Mason, UM) & arranged not to compete. But, in the 1930s, recalled Burnett, 'a strange fish began to ruffle the placid waters of this friendly pond . . . Earl Horter . . . swell chap . . . artist of repute . . . interested in making an Indian collection . . . Heye sold him several Plains pieces.'[3]

Horter was an auctioneer's delight. He wouldn't be outbid. According to Burnett, '. . . he got so excited at sales, he raised his own bids . . . [at] one sale in Philadelphia, he had three representatives buying for him and he bid against them.'[4]

'One morning George Heye came into my office at the Museum in a state of high excitement. He asked if I'd read the *Times* that morning. I hadn't. "Earl Horter is dead", he said. When I said, "Chief, that's too bad", he said, "Too bad, hell! He should have died years ago. Now I want you to drop everything, Ken. Get over to Germantown. See Mrs. Horter. Give her Treatment 19, with all the fringes. Let's see what we can make out of this."'[5]

Heye's strategy paid off. After the funeral, Mrs. Horter wrote to him, saying how fond her late husband had been of him & offering him the first opportunity to look over the collection. 'We went over to Germantown. I had a list of pieces Heye sold Horter and those where he outbid us. I packed them in the car, at a price about twenty cents on the dollar.

'On the way home, Heye was hitting it up about 70 miles an hour through New

Jersey, weaving in and out of traffic, crossing marked lanes, when a policeman pulled us over and asked for his license. Heye handed it to him. The cop looked at him, then looked at the back of the car and saw the material there. "You're not the Heye who has the big Indian collection in New York, are you?"

'Heye admitted he was. "Well, what do you know", said the policeman. "I collect Indian things myself."' So we sat by the roadside, collectors all — all except the State of New Jersey. It collected nothing.'[6]

JONES COLLECTION

Heye's first major purchase, 1906, was from a New Orleans widow. Her late husband, Joseph Jones, MD, left a vast collection. She circulated an illustrated brochure. George Pepper showed it to Heye.

Joseph Jones belonged to a remarkable family. His father, the Rev. Charles Colcock Jones (1804-1863), owned two Georgia plantations, each with slaves. The Reverend was said to be of 'radiant Christian character.' Known widely as the 'Apostle of the Blacks', he devoted his life to 'the moral elevation of the colored race.' One of his books, for 'the religious instruction of colored persons', enjoyed six editions. For this ecclesiastic duty, he was paid by other slave-owners who, in turn, were admired for their benevolence. Ill health confined him to home where he wrote. The whole family wrote. Publications by his sons Charles (1831-1893) & Joseph (1833-1896) fill shelves. Family correspondence is estimated at 50,000 surviving letters.[7]

Both sons served the Confederacy: Charles in artillery, Joseph first in cavalry, then medicine. Charles rose to Colonel, Joseph to Surgeon-Major. Like their father, both attended Princeton. Charles received an LLB from Harvard, Joseph an MD. After the War, Charles practiced law in New York. Then he returned to Georgia & founded the Confederate Survivors Association, serving as president until he died. He also helped found the American Anthropological Association, dedicated to reconciling archeology with the Bible. He served as its president, 1876-79.[8]

Joseph taught anatomy at Tulane Medical College. War experiences led him to focus on gangrene, sanitation, quarantine, yellow fever. In each, as author & advocate, he pioneered. It took him four years to get legislation passed allowing New Orleans police to enforce quarantine.

Prehistory attracted both brothers. Charles wrote *Antiquities of Tennessee*, 1873. Joseph, with Smithsonian financing, opened ancient graves in the Cumberland Valley. From this work came *Aboriginal Remains of Tennessee*, 1876. The Smithsonian also published his *American Vertebrata*, 1856.

Joseph's collection included artifacts from Egypt, Mexico, India, Peru. Somehow

46

he acquired the contents of a New Orleans museum, established in the early 19th century. His handwritten catalog (over 800 pages) is virtually useless. One can't tell what he dug, purchased, received.

He displayed all this at home, including the skulls. To these, he added his own drawings of those skulls, rendered in Gothic style. His widow wanted to tidy up. She sold Heye over 1000 southeastern antiquities for $4500.

SCHOFF COLLECTION

By 1953, the days of buying 1000 antiquities for $4500 were over. Heye's last major purchase, for $5000, involved a handful of 17th century Seneca objects.

Harry Schoff (1905-1970) grew up on a farm in upstate New York. It contained an Indian site. He soon located the graves. From 1936 to 1970, there & on neighboring sites, he opened 1123 graves. During the Depression (1929-1940), the WPA ran archeological digs. A former Heye archeologist, Donald Cadzow, hired Schoff to supervise crews in Pennsylvania. His work proved outstanding.

The Depression favored archeology. For one thing, it was non-competitive. Workers excavated, photographed, recorded. The Second War ended this, but not interest. Many dug on weekends. Schoff (blacksmith, cabinetmaker, country singer, occultist), dug whenever he could. For decades he collaborated with Charles Wray, a professionally trained archeologist. Wray opened 797 graves. What we know of Seneca protohistory comes largely from their efforts.[9]

Among the graves Schoff & Wray dug were those at Ganondagan & Fort Hill, in western New York. France hoped to re-establish their lucrative beaver trade. She saw these citadels as obstacles. The Marquis Denonville, with troops from Quebec, plus Indian allies from the West, 3000 in all, attacked, 1687. Ganondagan fell first.

But the attack on nearby Fort Hill was delayed for days as Indian allies looted Seneca graves for wampum. These same graves were reopened in the 1830s by blacksmiths seeking iron & clock smiths seeking copper. Church picnickers came next: women served food, while husbands dug for curios.

Wray & Schoff searched through this mess, patiently reconstructing Seneca history. Ultimately they assembled notes for about 3000 graves, plus thousands of specimens, all fragmentary, eroded, fragile, ugly, but documented. Most are now preserved in the Rochester Museum & Science Center.

Prior to 1960, the Seneca themselves led this research. Ely Parker, collaborator with Lewis Henry Morgan & Civil War general, donated specimens to the Board of Regents. His nephew, Arthur Parker, became New York State Archeologist; later Director, Rochester Museum; & the first President, Society of American Archeology.

Between 1917-1927, the MAI added 100,000 catalog cards. Every card averaged about three specimens. This meant about 30,000 objects a year. One week alone, 5000 were received.

After 1928, acquisitions slowed. Heye now chose not to use his own money. He sent telegrams to his staff, notifying them that they were no longer his concern. In Burnett's words, scholars 'dissipated during the months of 1931 and 1932.' One Trustee, Willard King, 'personally paid Marshall Saville $100 a month for a whole year.'[10]

Willem Wildschut's wife was shocked by this betrayal of her husband. She recalled 'that he locked the thousands of pages of his research [autobiography of Plenty Coups, a Crow chief] in a trunk and never mentioned the word "Indian" again.'[11]

'No one', writes Mason, 'with George Heye's drive, with his utter disregard for anything that intervened in his urge to build his collection even greater,' could stop him. 'About 1935-36, collecting again became a growing urge. . . . There were no funds for the scientific staff, perhaps, but there were an increasing number of collections being offered by others who themselves felt the pinch of the times, and Heye never rested a moment pursuing them and acquiring those of any importance.'[12]

During peak years, Heye acquired about 40 large, private collections. Most were poorly documented. He didn't care. Even when specimens were documented, he discarded records. What mattered, he reminded his staff, was the total.

1917: Dreyfus collection, California prehistory: $5000.

1918: Harley Stamp collection, Aleut & Eskimo material, much of it from caves.

Burns collection, Southwest archeology: $3000.

Tlingit & Kwakiutl, Fred Harvey: $4250.

1921: W.L. Bryant collection, Iroquois material: $1750.

1922: C.O. Borg collection, 113 *kachinas*: $1 each.

1924: The Heyes & Harmon Hendricks took a steamer to South America, returning on the same line. At Río, they purchased ethnographic material from one supplier; in Buenos Aires, from six. Much of the MAI collection from Argentina, Brazil, Peru & Paraguay, comes from this brief, casual trip.[13]

1925: Chandler collection. Mostly Great Lakes material: $7370.

1926: Ficker collection, Marajó material, Brazil: $5000.

Heye struck hard deals. In 1932, he was offered, by José Gayoso, Lima, a stunning collection of Peruvian gold & silver. The moment it arrived, he placed it in a vault. There it remained, 'on approval', for three years. Finally Heye offered $900, the price of the metals. Gayoso, rather than ship it back to Lima where no art market existed & metals sold by weight, reluctantly accepted. Burnett, who delighted in Heye's canniness, called the price 'bargain basement.'[14]

During the Depression, he acquired Alaskan Eskimo material from Henry Moses ($2850) & Alida Oayne Law ($1250); Peruvian material from the Schmidt-Pizzaro ($410) & Morkill ($525) collections; shields & covers from the Phoebe Apperson Hearst collection ($1250). All at rock bottom prices.

In 1936, he purchased, for $2500, plus shipping, the extensive William Fitzhugh collection, largely Plains Indian material. He put down $1000. Then he waited. Fitzhugh died. It required a court order to get the rest, plus a reminder from the estate attorney that shipping costs, $145.76, were due.[15]

COMPETITORS

Who were Heye's competitors? Museums of natural history in New York, Washington, Chicago. They took seriously the assembly & documentation of Indian artifacts. So did several smaller museums.

Private collectors were few. Farmers plowing fields often saved what they came upon. This led to fakes. Fake birdstones & bannerstones soon appeared, 1870-1910. A bit of that survives today at Indian auctions. Fakes sell for a fraction, but sell. A 'knapper', with booth, retouches blemished pieces. Attendees dress in boots, Stetsons, bolo ties, Indian jewelry. Lots often enjoy patriotic names. I recall a bannerstone called, 'American Glory.' There's even an annual *Who's Who in Indian Relics*.

Once hooked, the bug took on a life-time fascination. I recall a collector who later owned railroads. Still, what he really wanted was to corner the market in local Indian objects. To this end, he assembled a vast collection. The Depression ended whatever plans he had for a museum. He locked everything in a string of box cars on a railway siding. I never learned the outcome.

SOUVENIRS

Heye learned to spot fakes. He soon got rid of them, at a profit, of course. Souvenirs proved more troublesome. Fakes imitate. Souvenirs substitute. Conquered people sell images of their gods, their art, whatever, to their conquerors. It's the most available trade item they have. But, no matter how well concealed, souvenirs always bear the unmistakable mark of conquest.

'The first step after liquidating a people', writes the Czech historian Milan Hubi, 'is to erase its memory. Destroy its books, its culture, its history. Then have somebody write new books, manufacture a new culture, invent a new history. Before long the nation will begin to forget what it is and what it was. The world around will forget even faster.'

When one culture rides over another, it destroys forever a unique way of being. It leaves survivors humiliated, diminished, cast aside. In Scotland, after Culloden Moor, 1746, plaids were forbidden on penalty of death. England soon reversed this policy. She needed Scots to serve on the Thin Red Line, notably the Black Watch.

Tourists today are drawn to pipe bands, preferably in full uniform. They also buy tartans associated with specific clans. These are wholly 19th century creations, souvenirs.[16] Long before weaving, early tartans were assemblies of rectangular-shaped sheepskins, finger-painted on the skin side.

Heye's Golden Rule for field-collectors: Buy only the old. NO TOURIST MATERIAL.[17] Yet he ended up with many tourist items. He couldn't separate spurious from authentic, that is, made by Indians for Indians. One of the last exhibits the MAI mounted concerned Eskimo art. Nearly all were souvenirs.[18] Among Eskimos, Greenlandic carvers produced trolls for Danes; Henry Moore-like sculptures for Canadians; porn & scrimshaw for Alaskans; tableaux for Russians. Each reflected some fashion in the conquering culture.

American Indian souvenirs appeared in Brazil as early as the mid-16th century, including red feather dresses specifically commissioned for European curio cabinets. Souvenirs now constitute about 20% of the Heye collection. Not bad, considering that about half of all museum collections & nearly all private holdings are souvenirs.

ST. FRANÇOIS DE SALES

While collecting in French Canada, Heye learned of early Wabanaki records stored in the St. François de Sales Mission, Cornwall Island, Ontario. Most documents had been transferred elsewhere for safe-keeping, but the Mission retained several for liturgical use.

Heye arrived by chauffeured limousine, examined the documents, then asked if he might have them photographed. The resident missionary hesitated. Heye put down his gold watch & chain.

Years later, a Canadian linguist asked to see those documents. The missionary said that a big man in a chauffeured limousine left his watch & chain as security. Today it's difficult to determine which of the many Wabanaki documents, formerly in the Huntington Free Library, came from the St. François Mission.[19]

MÖLLER

Other acquisitions were curious. Major J. A. L. Möller collected Indian art & Mexican antiquities. His wife came from a wealthy family in Merida, Yucatan, with a successful exporting firm. The Möllers lived a half-hour's drive north of Heye's museum.

According to Burnett, Bill Stiles drove Heye there. While sitting in the living room, waiting for the good Major to mix drinks in the kitchen, Heye pointed to many of the Indian things hanging on the walls and said to Stiles, "Take them down and put them in the car."

'Stiles looked at him a minute, but he said, "Go ahead." When Möller returned, if he missed anything, he said nothing. He remained a good friend of the Museum until his death and gave us many things from Yucatan and Campeche. Dr. Heye and I drove out to the Möllers several times for lunch. If he made any further collections of Indian material, he kept them off the walls.'[20]

TRINKETS FOR NATIVES

New York (April 1, 1931)

Mrs. Herbert S. Dickey in her cabin, just before sailing on the S.S. Contoy with her husband at the head of their expedition into the interior of Venezuela. She shows some of the trinkets which she will take to the natives. The explorations are sponsored by the Museum of the American Indian, Heye Foundation, and other museums.

Fig. 1 shows northern Baffinland, as mapped by Nuqalluq.

Eskimo Map

Fig. 2 simplifies figure 1.

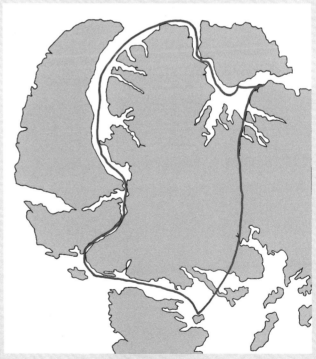

Fig. 3 shows a modern map of the same area.

Fig. 1 shows northern Baffinland, as mapped by Nuqallaq, headman at Pond Inlet.[1] Fig. 2, beside it, simplifies Fig. 1. Fig. 3, a modern map, covers the same area.

Nuqallaq's map concerns a sled journey jointly undertaken in 1913 by Albert Tremblay. Tremblay was an Able Seaman aboard a government patrol vessel, *Minnie Maud*, Captain Joseph E. Bernier.

Bernier collected ethnographic data, including Eskimo-drawn maps, for Franz Boas. But this chart had another origin. Tremblay allegedly claimed he reached Hudson Bay. Claude Vigneau, Quartermaster of the *Minnie Maud*, suspected exaggeration. He asked Nuqallaq to draw their route to see if Tremblay actually reached Hudson Bay.[1]

Tremblay accompanied the first sled. Nuqallaq drove the second sled. Whatever Tremblay claimed when he returned to the *Minnie Maud*, he made no such boast when he published *The Cruise of the Minnie Maud*, 1921, eight years later.[2] He said they went no farther than the northern part of the Melville Peninsula, far short of Hudson Bay.

THE ROUTE

Tremblay departed Arctic Bay, January 29, 1913, with Piunngittuq & his wife, Tutilik. Nuqallaq accompanied them with a second team.[3] They reached Igloolik, March 20th. Tremblay believed he was the first Westerner to visit Igloolik since Captain William Parry wintered there, 1822 & 1823. Apparently, he was unaware that Charles F. Hall visited Igloolik twice in the 1860s.[4]

After Parry departed, a shaman at Igloolik, jealous when his wife 'started to go around with some white people', asked a spirit helper to blow 'the ship away' & bring no others.[5] Tremblay sought to break this spell. He compared Igloolik to a shy animal he would kill. 'As he walked around the shoreline', he fired a pistol in the ground. This, he said, would break the shaman's spell. Once again, ships would visit Igloolik.[6]

Tremblay, with a new driver, Takkowah, crossed to the Melville Peninsula. There they visited Tasiujaq [Hall] Lake. Then they saw, but did not visit, Sarcpa Lake. They returned to Igloolik four days later.

From Igloolik, they departed April 15th on three sleds for Pond Inlet. En route, they met Nuqallaq. He refused to accept Tremblay's authority & continued on his own. Tremblay reached Pond Inlet, May 10th. Along the way, he named numerous geographical points for friends, heroes, himself.

Vigneau added details to Nuqallaq's map, presumably some at Nuqallaq's suggestion:

    1/ Salmon River

    2/ Bylot Island

    3/ Canada Point

    4/ Arctic Bay

    5/ where salmon are abundant

6/ chee two places where caribou are abundant; plus ampersands for their abundance elsewhere

7/ Xquimu 2 femme refers to Nuqallaq's account of a man marooned on an island as punishment for taking another man's two wives. There he found a dead whale, cut it up & hid the meat in rock crannies. One of his captors, believing him dead, returned to the island by kayak. Seeing nothing, he walked inland. The fugitive emerged from hiding, took the kayak & escaped. But the kayak capsized & he drowned. The other man, not finding the meat, starved.

MANSLAUGHTER

Nuqallaq & two others were later charged with killing Robert Janes, a trader at Crauford, Baffin Island. Janes, known locally as Sakirmiaq (a corruption of the English 'Second Mate'),[7] quarreled with nearly everyone, threatened, attacked. Clearly, he was out of control, possibly insane. Vigneau said he cheated the Eskimo. Presumably he referred to Naqitarvik, from whom Janes stole furs. He also stole furs & ivory from Bernier. The Court might easily have justified the killing.

Instead, it acquitted Alleetah for lack of evidence & found Oorooreangnah guilty, but recommended clemency. Nuqallaq was convicted of manslaughter & sentenced to ten years at hard labor. At Stony Mountain Penitentiary, Manitoba, he contracted tuberculosis. Released after eighteen months, he returned to Pond Inlet & soon died.[8] A flu outbreak followed, then TB, with many deaths.

Elders at Pond Inlet (1989-1994) recalled how, when the First War started, Janes tried to return by ship. They looked after him, fed him, even made plans to take him by sled to Chesterfield Inlet. But, increasingly, his behavior became abnormal. He tried to kill Umik, Nuqallaq's father. A reluctant Nuqallaq was selected to kill him.[9]

Elders also mentioned how Nuqallaq abused two wives. When he & his first wife hunted alone, 'she … lost a lot of weight' (starved) & committed suicide. He remarried someone much younger. She bore 'a facial scar … caused by him.' The elders attributed his harsh sentence to abuse.[10]

MAI

How the ethnologist Frank Speck met the Quartermaster Claude Vigneau, I don't know. It may have been in the Far North. Speck bought from him various artifacts, including the map, 3 stone pipes (one belonging to Nuqallaq) & 2 sealskin parkas (one belonging to Nuqallaq). Speck scribbled '25 Sep 1923' on the map & deposited the lot at the MAI. They were accessioned in 1924.

The catalog doesn't identify which parka or which pipe belonged to Nuqallaq. Heye sold one pipe, 12/7211-2, to William Shirley Fulton, 1943. Apparently the map was never accessioned & may have been discarded. Fortunately, Speck published it, along with the account of the man abandoned.[11]

CHAPTER 4   Field-collecting

Heye assembled a staff like no other, anywhere, ever. For varying periods, these men worked full-time for him:

Theodore de Booy	Amos Oneroad
E. K. Burnett	William C. Orchard
E. J. Bush	George P. Pepper
Donald A. Cadzow	Edward Sapir
James B. Clemens	Foster H. Saville
Edward F. Coffin	Marshall H. Saville
William C. Farabee	Louis Schellbach
Melvin R. Gilmore	Alanson Buck Skinner
Mark R. Harrington	Frank G. Speck
Frederick Hodge	William Stiles
Samuel K. Lothrop	Charles Turbyfill
William Mechling	Wilson Wallace
Jesse L. Nusbaum	Willem Wildschut
Bruno Oetteking	A. Hyatt Verrill

Most were young, talented. Many were mavericks. One night in South Dakota, Alanson Buck Skinner (1885-1925) had drunk too much. A shaman's drumming got on his nerves. He brought the drum down over the shaman's head, splitting the hide & pinning the drummer's arms. The Indians understood. They accepted him. A few years later, he died among them, in a car accident.[1]

A hundred years ago to finance field-collecting, explorers asked several museums for advances, then divided the resulting collection. Heye regularly advanced such funds, especially to individuals on leave from other institutions. He might then offer permanent employment, with pension. Pepper, Saville, Harrington, Hodge, Skinner &

Cadzow were among the first to join up, along with various technicians: Bush, Coffin, Orchard, Turbyfill.

Museums generally distinguish between staff-collectors & field-collectors. The latter lived in remote areas & collected locally. All were self-trained. Without their efforts, American ethnology would have another history.

Ethnologists, like bartenders, tolerate human eccentricity — it's their livelihood. Heye, Wallace wrote, tolerated anthropologists.[2] When he learned, by chance, that one of his archeologists, who was supposed to be in Panama, was actually in Peru, he remained calm: ' … the more you deal with Verrill, the more remarkable some of his actions seem to be.'[3]

G.T. EMMONS (1852-1945)

One of Heye's early suppliers was Lt. George T. Emmons, USN. Emmons collected principally among the Tlingit of Alaska, where he was stationed. Most of what he collected went to the AMNH. Yet some of Heye's finest pieces came from Emmons, often directly from shaman's graves. The Tlingit watched Emmons take them. Yet he enjoyed their life-long friendship. This puzzled me until I read that Tlingit masks might be owned by successive shamans. Masks weren't abandoned on graves to rot, but placed there to be retrieved by those who, having studied & sacrificed, qualified as guardians.

Emmons qualified. Obviously, he wasn't the Tlingits' first choice. But, at that moment, he was their only choice. I recall a photograph of a dying Vietnamese woman handing her infant to a Western journalist. This wasn't the way she wanted life to be, but she desperately wanted her child to survive.

Tlingit elders transferred sacred treasures to Emmons, whom they trusted. They believed that powers within those objects & truths within those myths could survive anything except neglect. They had no illusions about their own children. Emmons was often their only listener.

Yes, yes, I know — all those stories about theft & chicanery, stories beloved by journalists. Some are true. But reality was even sadder. The real problem was one culture riding over another. Emmons saved what he could. He served as a surrogate tribal elder when those offices stood empty. He never intended to deprive anyone, least of all the Tlingit, of their heritage. He sought only to preserve. Without his efforts, what would now survive?

ADAMS H. TWITCHELL (1872-1949)

Born in Vermont, Twitchell joined the gold rush, tried mining, then trading. He arrived in Bethel, Alaska, with his wife, a Yup'ik woman from a tundra village, having sailed 80 miles up the Kuskokwim River, with trade goods. There they remained until 1916, when they moved upriver to herd reindeer.

'Although he earned his living as a trader, Twitchell was a self-made scientist with an avid interest in natural history. He collected ornithological specimens for the Smithsonian and was a recognized authority on local flora and fauna.'[4]

Twitchell had eight children. 'In latter years', wrote his son Ben, 'when he had gone into the reindeer business and had to travel by foot between the reindeer range and the towns that were his market, he would not hesitate to let the pack horses go on alone or stop to feed while he unpacked his insect net and chased after a butterfly specimen that some museum or collector wanted. . . . He received orders . . . from as far away as England. Biologists and botanists sought him out.'[5]

As I understand the story, the Yup'ik sometimes used Twitchell's warehouse for dance ceremonies, over the protests of a local missionary. In a letter to George Gordon, he wrote: 'I attended one dance just to get the masks and information, and went to another and stayed a week until it finished.'[6]

The mask opposite represents the 'muskrat god, Andlu (probably *anlu*, "the hole through which the muskrat emerged from its den", from *ane-*, "go out").' Twitchell wrote, 'When turned face downward the mask represents a muskrat house. When face upward the rats can be pulled through the hole in the house, the way they come out in the spring. The white discs on the stick represent bubbles. The white face has four teeth, the same as muskrats, and is a member of the same family. He furnishes plenty of rats in the spring, so their skins may be used for clothing.'[7] Hanging pieces below may be water hemlock which muskrats eat.[8]

'Twitchell had the naturalist's penchant for recording detail.... This may seem a minor accomplishment, but in all the thousands of Yup'ik masks dating to the turn of the century, only those collected by Twitchell and, to a lesser extent, Jacobsen, are accompanied by such information. Twitchell's years in Bethel and his Yup'ik wife likely gave him the necessary access and sensitivity. . . .'[9]

FRANK G. SPECK (1881-1950)

Speck's health led his family to place him, when he was seven, in rural Connecticut, with a distant relative, a Mohegan-Pequot widow. From her, he learned Algonkian, herbal lore & love of nature.[10]

60

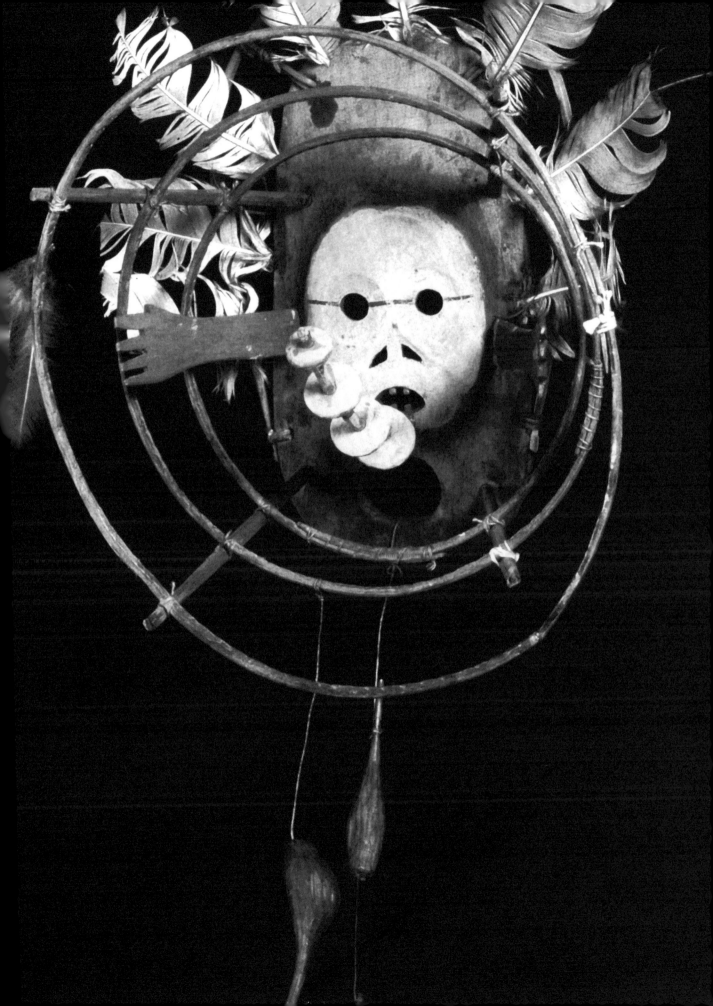

As an undergraduate at Columbia, he co-authored three articles on Algonkian with Professor J. Dyneley Prince, noted philologist.[11] His first Mohegan specimens entered the Heye collection in 1905. He studied under Franz Boas, did fieldwork in Oklahoma Indian Territory & then accepted a job with Heye at the University Museum, Philadelphia, 1907. In time, he established the Anthropology Department, University of Pennsylvania.

His office resembled an 18th century curio cabinet, complete with specimens, living & dead. Designed as a chapel, then for a literary society, it enjoyed Gothic windows with high ceilings. Books lined three walls, floor to ceiling. Most had broken spines, with tabs sticking out. Down the center ran a meeting-house table, a bench on either side. Three tables, each with ancient typewriter, served faculty & students alike. Specimens filled corners, walls, chairs. Snakes & turtles sunned in glass cages. Once, briefly, an arctic fox, unfriendly, hid behind a leaking radiator. Students, Indian delegations, visiting scholars, ate there daily.

The door to this menagerie was best opened with caution. Speck used it to test weapons. Darts & spears protruded through splintered panels.

He had a superb ear, moving from language to language like a train switching tracks. He never paid informants. He feared, rightly, commercializing ethnology. But he sent endless gifts: beads, hides, whatever was needed to maintain tribal traditions. He shared authorship. Today, it's easy to forget what it meant, 100 years ago, for a tribal elder to be a published author.

Physically he was short, compact, with baleful eyes. He spoke little. He never complained. He was immensely kind. He wasted no thought on politics, sports, newspapers, faculty meetings & certainly no money on clothes.

Above all, he loved fieldwork, tribe after tribe, Labrador to Louisiana. He was particularly interested in Old World traditions surviving among American Indians. Two graduate students shared those interests. They soon joined the Department of Anthropology. For his MA & PhD theses, A.I. Hallowell compared Old & New World fishnets,[12] then Bear Ceremonialism.[13] D.S. Davidson compared Old & New World snowshoes.[14]

Speck recorded over 450 texts, ceremonies, myths. Brief holidays meant nearby tribes. On one occasion, a group returned from the Nanticoke in two cars, agreeing to meet in a Dover restaurant. The second car was delayed. The others decided not to wait. Vladimir Fewkes scribbled a note: 'We have the head. Do you have the body? Meet at the rendezvous.' The waitress promised not to read the note.

When the second group arrived, they were handcuffed & jailed until morning, when the father of one of them, a Philadelphia detective, explained.

Good ethnographic collections often contain specimens commissioned for study. Heye's collection includes — or once included — specimens Speck commissioned. These might be, say, Naskapi miniature models of traps. When the Oklahoma Delaware offered Speck an anthropomorphic drumstick, he urged them to keep it, but make new ones, for their own use & for museums. He commissioned feather robes from Indian women in Virginia. They'd never seen one. Feather robes hadn't been made for centuries. Speck hoped they would pool traditional knotting-tying techniques. Heye was vastly amused.

Speck gave up on him. I recall a morning in his office when he handed me a letter just received. In it, Heye spoke of the old crowd, now mostly gone. He said he no longer traveled. But, if Speck came to New York, it would mean much to him to see Speck again. I returned the letter. He dropped it in the trash.

MARK R. HARRINGTON (1882-1971)

No one added more specimens to the MAI collection than Mark Harrington. Excluding those sold, traded or missing, they now number 54,440.[15] He wrote 14 books, excavated in 8 States & left ethnographic accounts of 42 American Indian tribes.

He couldn't wait to get into the field. At 17, he joined the staff of the AMNH, where he remained four years. Then he returned home, took a B.S. degree at Michigan (his father taught there) & an M.A. under Boas at Columbia. In 1911, he joined the staff of the University Museum, Philadelphia. A few years later, Heye put him on salary. He remained with Heye until 1928, when he went to the Southwest Museum, Los Angeles. He retired at 82.

William Sturtevant, a Smithsonian ethnologist, asked Harrington if his Heye field notes survived. They did, on file at the Southwest Museum. Harrington happily shared them.

It would be a simple matter to reunite these specimens & notes.

SAMUEL KIRKLAND LOTHROP (1892-1965)

Samuel Kirkland Lothrop bore the name of his great-grandfather, *the* leading Unitarian minister of his time. It was a distinguished New England family, in the Brahmin, intellectual tradition.

He grew up in Massachusetts & Puerto Rico where his father had sugar interests. He attended Groton & Harvard; then took a doctorate in archeology, 1921. His first dig was Pecos, New Mexico, sponsored by Phillips Academy, Andover, 1915. Then came digs in Puerto Rico, Guatemala, Honduras, 1915-17. During both World Wars, he spied for the U.S. Archeologists, especially those of patrician background, often did, spying being a sub-branch of archeology.

In 1924, Lothrop joined Heye's staff. Heye sent him first to Kechiba:wa, New Mexico, then Central America, Tierra del Fuego, Argentina, Peru, etc, etc. According to Gordon Willey, 'It was the most productive period in his career and, in many ways, the happiest.'[16]

In 1929, he married Eleanor Bachman, a woman of talent & wealth. The two were said to be very handsome. George Heye accompanied them on their honeymoon.[17] After Heye returned to New York, Eleanor Lothrop wrote:

'I used to think that Mr. Heye took a fiendish pleasure in picking out the most villainous spots in Chile for us to cover. Whenever we were at our lowest ebb, I would torture myself by imagining him comfortably ensconced in his magnificent apartment with a box of especially imported Havana cigars and some newly acquired first editions. Or sitting in one of New York's luxurious restaurants, washing down breasts of guinea hen *sous cloche* with a bottle of Montrachet, 1911. "Poor Lothrops", he would undoubtedly be saying, as the waiter filled his glass for the third time.'[18]

Employment with Heye ended, 1930. Lothrop moved to the Peabody Museum, Harvard. By then he was one of America's most respected anthropologists, equally at home in archeology & ethnology. In Willey's words: 'he had no peer.'[19] His personal library also had no peer. He willed it to Harvard.

Donald Cadzow grew up in the North where, I believe, his uncle was a fur trader. Heye sent him off with Turbyfill to dig rock shelters in the Ozarks:

'One day Cadzow and I dug up a little child's mummy and packed it out through a cornfield . . . in the second row of corn we walked straight into a man making corn liquor. We walked right on past with our mummy as though we didn't notice anything. But HE noticed.

'We moved on up the river in our canoe a little afterwards, and sure enough I see this man standing up on a bluff with overhauls and a black slouch hat and a damn Winchester, and then I hear poomp, poomp, poomp and the damn bullets hitting the water beside us, and I yelled, "Holy God, don't shoot. We're archeologists."'[20]

No one ever again mistook Cadzow for anything other than an archeologist. He dressed in riding breeches & boots. He answered to 'Doctor.' Even Turbyfill called him 'Dr. Cadzow.' Heye sent him on digs from the Southwest Desert to Baffinland.

When MAI employment ended, 1929, Cadzow talked the Franklin Automobile Company into a Canadian expedition, featuring an air-cooled Franklin. Two Australian brothers joined him. One was identified as Robert Rymill, having 'recently completed his anthropological studies at Cambridge University . . . champion marksman' & his younger brother, John Rymill, a 6'4", 250-pound boxer.

Half their funds ($6000) went for expenses, the other half for specimens. Cambridge University Museum of Archaeology and Anthropology (CUMAA) now has approximately '500 pieces . . . known as the Rymill collection.' In addition, there are 33 b&w photographs, 20 minutes of film footage, newspaper clippings & correspondence.[21] Neither the British Museum nor CUMAA record any fauna.[22]

The expedition took off from Syracuse, New York, crossed the continent at record speed & spent several days 'with the Bungi Indians, studying their life and customs. The boys were initiated into one of the ancient Indian societies, the Mediwin, or Medicine society. This was an all-night ceremony . . . performed to the accompaniment of the water drum, which throbbed incessantly. The sacred, stone smoking pipe was passed many times and, as the boys were not smokers, this was a true test of their interest in aboriginal life.'[23]

With 'cowboy hats and buckskin coats . . . we looked more like trappers out of the north than traveling scientists.' The northernmost visit took them to the Saulteaux, in mosquito-filled muskeg, reached via wagon trails, only to find themselves unwelcome, among people 'hating the white man with a fierce, vindictive passion.

'Separated from the rest of civilization by 200 miles of swamp and wilderness and surrounded by savages . . . my position was unenviable. . . . With the rest of my party in the hills and bitter hostility smoldering just beneath the surface on all sides, I was forced to put my trust in the instant availability and reliability of the car, and to work always with the possibility of flight uppermost in my plans.'

While his companions hunted, Cadzow allegedly collected 700 ethnographic specimens.[24] 'Fifteen days later . . . loaded down with trophies, we returned to Prince Albert. A few days were spent among the Wapeton Sioux north of that city . . . a short trip to Emma Lake to hunt Elk and we again returned to Prince Albert and shipped our specimens back to England.

'After a sight-seeing trip to Banff . . . we crossed the Rocky Mountains and dropped down into . . . the Kootenai trail. Worked among the Kootenai Indians and then moved south and east through the Crows Nest Pass. . . . Here we spent several days among the Piegan Indians and hunting Mountain sheep. . . . It was only a step . . . to Yellowstone Park . . . then south to Cheyenne, where the expedition officially ended … [We] returned to civilization.'[25]

Cadzow then joined the Pennsylvania Historical Commission. He first supervised Depression-era digs, often with large crews. Appointments were political, but somehow Junius Bird & Frank Siebert joined these crews. Both became outstanding anthropologists.

Cadzow rose rapidly within the Commission to Executive Director. By 1940, still with the Historical Commission, he ran the State's political patronage system.

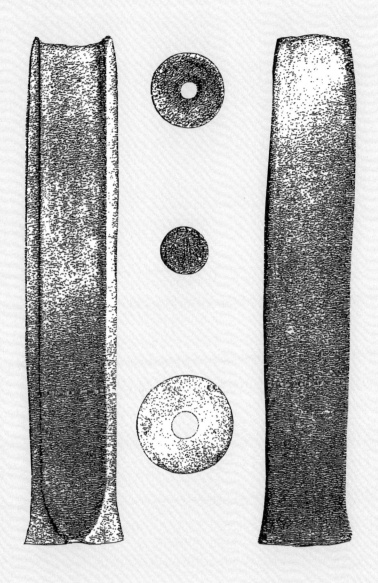

Champlain Site

From 1933-1935, the MAI excavated an ancient cemetery in Vermont. The work was directed by Godfrey J. Olsen, financed by Stephen H. P. Pell. Olsen had earlier excavated for Heye in Haiti, with another patron.

The Vermont site occupied the bank of a small bay formed by the mouth of East Creek & Lake Champlain. Directly across this creek rises Mt. Independence, a landmark on the Vermont shore & the source of distinctive, black chert used to fashion cache blades.

Olsen, with a small crew of volunteers, first laid out a grid. The site, they quickly found, enjoyed multiple occupations: colonial to ancient, but primarily Eastern Woodland village & associated cemetery. In pits 'crammed full of rubbish', they found identifiable bones of deer, elk, moose, beaver, muskrat, squirrel, wolf, fox, dog, various birds, several kinds of fish, freshwater mussel shells, hard clam shells, as well as beech & hickory nuts, charred corn, squash seeds, acorns & walnuts.

Today's MAI holdings include only hickory & beech nuts, carbonized acorns & freshwater mussel shells.

BURIALS

Before the first season closed, Olsen located 12 burials. All lay deep in clay subsoil, below a surface deposit of sand. The first indication of a burial might be green stains from copper ornaments. In 1934, Olsen found 36 more graves. In 1935, 4. Total: 52.

Burials were basin-shaped, often lined with elm bark. In several, beneath the bark lining, occurred a thin layer of hardened clay. All graves contained quantities of red ochre. Ochre concentrations often lay adjacent to or over artifacts, suggesting they were originally placed in hide or bark containers.

Skeletons were cremated or bundle buried. A crematory was located the first year: carefully molded, shallow, roughly 3'x 5'. It was cut out of, then shaped in hard pan clay, which covered part of the site. In this charcoal-filled basin lay 80 cache blades (a popular funeral offering), plus a birdstone (probably a spear-thrower weight). The MAI now has 73 of these cache blades: at least 70 are of Mt. Independence chert.

A large, adjacent pit, 9 feet deep, contained 1.5 feet of burnt human bones, intermingled with quantities of charred oak branches. But no artifacts.

However, the 52 graves produced an extraordinary number of exotic burial offerings, including 27 blocked-end tubes, 19 of which came from Ohio Valley. How do we explain their presence in Vermont? One theory is that a network of traders & proselytizers converted eastern tribes to a burial cult that stretched from Virginia to Gaspé.

Among the imported rituals of this cult were offerings to accompany the dead: native copper from Lake Superior, marine shells from the coast, slate gorgets, cache blades, birdstones, boatstones & fire-clay tubular pipes.

Imagine bamboo cut through one node, then, moving upward, cut just below the next node. Carve this from southern Ohio limestone *&* you have the most diagnostic trait of the Adena culture, circa 300 BC-AD 300.

Tubes served as smoking pipes. A few had small, round stones inside, one to a tube. Carbonized matter, presumably tobacco, remained in many. To smoke: insert tobacco, light, add stone, then suck at the smaller opening. Identical pipes, made from bamboo, are smoked today in several parts of the world, especially in modern New Guinea.

I know of no surviving, prehistoric blocked-end tube made from bamboo from Ohio. But a single section of cane, *Arundinaria gigantea* (Watt), 9"x 1", wrapped in native sheet silver, survived in a Pennsylvania mound.[1] In the Mississippi Valley, this species reaches southern Ohio.

UNIQUE SITE

What made this site so remarkable? It enjoyed the distinction of being the first, possibly the only, Eastern Adena site opened with care. All others, without exception, were looted *&* their finds scattered. Compare an archeological site to a disappearing manuscript that can only be read once. Godfrey Olsen went to great lengths to record *&* preserve. He removed entire blocks of earth to keep everything *in situ*. This included small piles of tiny, pressure-retouch flakes of Onondaga chert, carefully deposited with other mortuary offerings. These were 'produced by re-sharpening some of the large, imported bifaces to insure their optimum condition at the time they were buried. . . . small piles . . . layered with red ochre.'[2]

The only other concentration of Adena-Hopewell material, outside of the Ohio heartland, is on the Delmarva Peninsula. Dr. Stephen Loring writes: 'I think the Mt. Independence chert quarries figured significantly in the [Vermont] story.'[3] Did that chert supply other Adena communites in New England?

MINDLESS DESTRUCTION

Olsen turned everything over to Heye. Heye cataloged what he wanted *&* discarded the rest, including Olsen's field notes, sketches, maps. MAI's only record, the catalog, lists 40, not 52, burials *&* little else. Heye was recklessly irresponsible.

Fifty years later, Stephen Loring assembled the few surviving scraps: newspaper accounts, a lecture, whatever. He mentioned 'personality conflicts.'[4] Nothing personal. Professional. Olsen, whom I knew, was furious. Better to have left the site untouched than this mindless destruction.[5]

CHAPTER 5   A Killing

Let me draw freely from the NMAI Archives, principally Box OC 121:1-4, starting with this letter:

1915

Dear Turbyfill:

The pipe is one of the best I have ever seen.
Do not mention this to anyone as I have shown
it to no one yet. I rather feel you would make
a killing by doing some work where you are.

George Heye

Heye wrote from England. Turbyfill received the letter in Murphy, North Carolina, where he was opening a burial mound. He selected that site, he said, because 'of a Miss Dickey at Murphy who ran the best restaurant in the United States: five meats for breakfast.'[1]

According to Turbyfill, Heye's advice paid off: 'That's just what we made — a killing. Worlds and worlds of pots, 1500 years old, and skeletons, shell beads, gaming stones.'

The word 'killing', a Wall Street favorite, appears repeatedly in Heye's confidential correspondence. He used it to describe treasure acquired for little, preferably nothing, secretly if possible. He didn't acquire to possess. Possession meant responsibility. Objects once acquired, lost luster. Like the seducer who shuns marriage, Heye found satisfaction in conquest alone. He reveled in it. Details survive as marginalia he added to letters before filing. They make amazing reading. I imagine him chortling each time he did somebody in, royally.

A 'great killing' required bulk. That meant existing collections. It's pure myth that Heye stripped reservations, leaving locals naked. By 1900, little remained on reservations, save in the Far North & even there, pickings were slim. Souvenirs already dominated. Stories that 'a fat man from New York bought the place out', aren't so. Nearly all great pieces had long since been collected. Heye knew where many were. Some cluttered the homes of widows, anxious to tidy up. The best were in museums, often in storage.

Heye's greatest 'killing' became known to generations of American archeologists as The Great Robbery. Junius Bird called it 'a sale as devious as anything on record.'[2] Another curator called it 'the greatest scandal in the history of American archeology and ethnology.'[3] Heye pulled off this heist at the Academy of Natural Sciences (ANS), Philadelphia, 1929. In one swoooooop, he got 35,000 specimens, including treasures beyond value. He paid $7000 for everything.

Philadelphia had in place a general agreement that its main museums would trade or donate holdings outside their special areas. The Academy's President, Effingham Morris, a banker, ignored this understanding. He decided, independently, to limit the Academy's operations to natural science & store the rest. To implement this decision, he appointed a protégé, Charles Cadwalader, as Managing Director. He informed neither Board nor staff of his plans.

How Heye found out, I don't know, but he did. In less than six weeks, he had what he wanted. He hoped to remain out of sight, but the moment he collided with H. Newell Wardle, he became visible. Harriet Wardle, a tiny scholar, dedicated thirty years to the Academy's archeological collections. She fought back. The local press featured the story as comedy: butterfly vs. Sumo. She stood no chance.

CLARENCE B. MOORE (1852-1936)

Heye first focused on the collection of Clarence B. Moore, a Philadelphia rail magnate. Miss Wardle called it 'the finest, most comprehensive and best documented assemblage of Indian antiquities from the southern states.'[4] She understated. Now its wonders were to be replaced by stuffed sheep & goats.

From 1891-1918, Moore undertook, at personal expense, major excavations in the southeastern United States. His field notes total 8707 pages. He then published, privately, 19 illustrated, bound reports & distributed these free of charge. He asked only that receipt be acknowledged. When none came from one scholar, Moore sent him a self-addressed postcard with instructions: If received, write 'yes'; if not received, write 'no'; if not wanted, write 'nit.' It was acknowledged.[5]

Moore was in Florida when Heye advised him of Morris's decision. Heye proposed transferring everything to his museum. As compensation, he would offer the Academy $10,000 'for having looked after' the collection.

Moore was very upset, but felt he had no alternative. He was 77, without heirs. If he said, 'No', his collection would disappear into storage. He agreed. Heye, fearing the

Academy might 'try to deal with the University Museum', asked for first refusal.

Heye wrote to Moore about meeting Cadwalader: 'energetic young man . . . [doesn't] claim to know anything about museums . . . wishes to run the Academy from a business point of view, which makes it easier for us to deal with them.'

Heye next met with Morris who, he wrote, 'was also desirous of getting rid of the archeology at the Academy', but feared criticism for allowing 'a collection that some people might consider valuable' going elsewhere. I told him no one needs to know about it until long after the deal had been consummated.'

Cadwalader said Philadelphia was 'in some ways a small town.' He feared adverse publicity & asked how the collection could be 'gotten out.' Heye suggested storing it locally (at his expense), leaving it there for a few months, then taking it to New York 'without anyone knowing.' Inquiries could be truthfully answered: 'in storage.'

'This idea pleased Morris. He asked me what we would pay for [your] collection . . . I told him you and I agreed [on] $10,000 . . . he seemed satisfied. He wondered [if we were] interested in obtaining the rest of the American [Indian material] in the building. I said, "Certainly."'

OTHER COLLECTIONS

Beneath the Moore display cases, in locked but accessible drawers, were major collections, including Robert Peary's Polar Eskimo material from northwest Greenland, as well as Major John Bourke's material from the Southwest Desert. According to Louis Agassiz, Samuel G. Morton's assembly of 600 human skulls, known in scientific centers as the American Golgotha, was 'worth the trip to America just to see.'

As U.S. Ambassador to Mexico, R. H. Lamborn acquired outstanding pre-Columbian pieces & endowed them, at the Academy, for $500,000, an immense sum then. Amos Gottschall, a patent medicine peddler, swapped 'tonics' to Indians for over 50,000 artifacts, the 'best' of which, numbering 3793, he donated to the Academy. He valued these at $50,000.

The largest collection came on loan from the American Philosophical Society (APS).[6] The APS accessioned their first specimen in 1772. Donors' names stood out: Biddle, Dickinson, Barton, Jefferson. The collection was a national legacy.

Early donors contributed single specimens. Collections followed: Haldeman (10,000); Pointdett (2800); Peale (1800). In 1891, the entire APS collection was 'placed for safekeeping' in the Academy's fireproof building. It remained there until Heye arrived.

Miss Wardle asked Cadwalader if the cases went with the specimens. 'Who', he asked, 'told you the Moore collection was sold'?

'I had it from Mr. Heye.'

'You were not supposed to talk to Mr. Heye — Mr. Heye was not supposed to say anything about it', Cadwalader warned: 'Silence or immediate dismissal.'[7]

Heye & the Academy signed a tentative agreement. He then telegraphed Moore: PLEASE FURNISH MY MAN UTLEY . . . WITH KEYS TO THE UPRIGHT CASES . . . MISS WARDLE PUTTING EVERY OBSTACLE IN OUR WAY.

When Utley unlocked the cases, Miss Wardle resigned, protesting a decision 'made without the knowledge of all Board members . . . loss of these priceless collections . . . breach of faith with the past . . . menace to the future . . . secretly negotiated . . . clandestine removal.'[8] All true, except 'clandestine.' Someone alerted the press.

Philadelphia newspapers featured the story. Heye told Moore what happened: ' . . . hectic day . . . succession of reporters . . . phone calls . . . visits from old women who had never known the Academy was on the map, and look as if they had not been in town for several generations. Unfortunately, no attractive young flappers [provided] a spot of brightness . . . Miss Wardle reached the Academy sometime before [8:30 a.m.] and took a number of Lamborn specimens . . . but not any of your material . . . this transaction has really aroused Philadelphia.'[9]

Heye took everything to New York. There he selected what he wanted, then returned the rest to the Academy. He left it, according to Miss Wardle, 'piled, loose, unpacked, indiscriminately, on the floor of the old museum', now a warehouse.[10] It remained there until 1942 when it was transferred to the University Museum. The collection that suffered most came from Samuel Haldeman, a famous naturalist. Haldeman excavated local sites, documenting everything. Heye had no interest in sherds, bones, broken tools, the very stuff of archeology. Without consulting Haldeman's records, he simply chose what caught his eye. He did the same with the other collections.

Cadwalader advised the press that only the Moore collection had been transferred. Everything else had 'been merely loaned [to the MAI] on the usual terms of study.' The press didn't buy this. Negative coverage continued. The uproar embarrassed the Academy. Heye seized on their embarrassment. The moment he had what he wanted, he summoned Cadwalader & the Academy's counsel to New York & dictated a new agreement.

He had given the Academy $10,000 for Moore's collection, plus $5000 for everything else. Now he demanded $5000 back. Then, as he wrote Moore, 'We take out from the other collection what we require for study and exhibition purposes (this means returning to them about 50%, stuff which is of the worst kind of junk and which he would have thrown away). This is returned at their expense and in addition they are to pay us $3000 for conditioning the pieces we keep here. The loan is indefinite which means the material in all probability will remain here forever.'[11]

In short, Heye paid the Academy $7000 for everything he kept. In a letter to Moore, he confided, ' . . . you are the only one I can tell about [this settlement] . . . I consider it my greatest triumph.'[12]

The official agreement stated that the Academy lent collections owned by them 'for such time as may be reasonably required' for exhibition, conservation & study. Heye guaranteed to use them 'only for [these] purposes' & to indemnify the Academy against claims. He further promised to catalog all loan specimens consecutively: 16/7000 to 16/8090 so 'there will be no trouble' in identifying pieces that might be challenged.

JEFFERSON GIFT

The APS threatened court action. Heye resorted to his usual ploy. He returned what he didn't want, kept what he wanted & left disputed pieces un-cataloged. There were many. One was a stone statue from Tennessee, donated by Thomas Jefferson to the Society in 1791. Jefferson believed it represented 'a woman in the first moments of parturition.'[13]

More likely, it belongs to a genre of paired male & female figures, each representing a Clan or Class Founder, shown in ceremonial posture. About a hundred such figures survive. Heye already had better examples, especially 0/7277, a male figure acquired from the Joseph Jones estate, 1906. But he liked the Jeffersonian connection. He left the statue un-cataloged. Someone later numbered it 19/2495.

Two cards bear that number. A temporary card, hand-numbered, reads:

> Idol of stone.
> Squatting position.
> Aztec People.
> Mexico. 9½ ins.

A second card, machine-numbered, says:

> Stone figure of seated woman,
> Trigg County, Kentucky,
> William M. Fitzhugh Collection.

Only the height is accurate. The figure isn't Aztec, never came from Mexico or Kentucky & never belonged to William Fitzhugh. Heye bought Fitzhugh's Plains Indian collection in 1936, seven years after he acquired the Jefferson statue. 19/2495 is a 1960 number. Heye died in 1957. Conceivably, he post-dated both cards, but that's unlikely. 'The Chief' cast a long shadow.

According to Burnett & Stiles, Heye kept (in a locked drawer) accurate records elsewhere falsified. What adds plausibility to this charge is Heye's statement that the true location of an Aleutian cave lay in that locked drawer. According to Burnett & Stiles, Heye destroyed that file on his last visit to the museum.

SCIENCE VS. ANS

The unofficial record appeared in *Science*, 1929, signed H. Newell Wardle: 'shame . . . ancient and honorable institution . . . misguided trustees, chosen for their business ability . . . without asking expert advice . . . wreck a scientific department . . . shakes the foundation of confidence in every institution in America.'[14]

In 1964, Heye's successor, Ken Burnett, commented: 'This little lady [H. Newell Wardle] is now dead, but even when she was well into her 90s, she never met a member of the Heye Foundation, or heard its name mentioned, without a glitter in her eye and a tightening of her lips.'[15]

The formal record appears in the *Academy of Natural Sciences Yearbook*, 1929: 'After repeated requests from Clarence B. Moore, donor, the Trustees sanctioned removal of his archaeological collection to the Museum of the American Indian, New York. All of this material related to the Indians of the Southeastern United States, none of it having to do solely with local tribes. During the year the Academy loaned other collections to this museum, in conformance with the courtesies customary among institutions.'

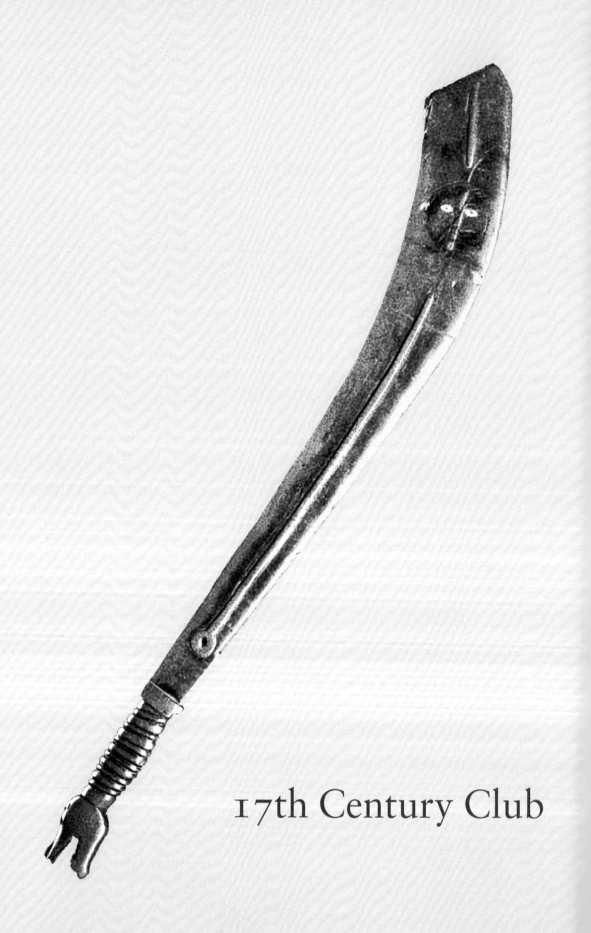

17th Century Club

Few 17th century Indian objects from New England survive. Even fewer possess credible proveniences. It's a delight, then, to find an object preserved & honored within one family for over 300 years.

In 1675, John King, Northampton, Massachusetts, was 18 at the outbreak of the King Philip's War. Hungry Indians raided herds, attacked settlements, burned Deerfield. The English, who outnumbered them 2 to 1, tried to exterminate them.[1] Indian refugees fled west. Several hundred congregated on both banks of the Connecticut River, near a fifty-foot waterfall. When spring came, they fished, planted.

On May 15th, a soldier held captive there, escaped & reached Hatfield town, twenty miles away. He named other captives & reported new Indian settlements. He said Deerfield's abandoned fields were newly planted & stolen cattle penned there. He reported that Indian camps were unguarded & estimated no more than 60-70 warriors.

Three days later, some 134-150 volunteers, including John King, assembled at Hatfield under Captain William Turner. Each brought his knapsack & doglock (early flintlock). Most were mounted. At dusk, they took the trail to Deerfield & rode silently through its charred ruins. Beyond the town, they shunned the usual ford & crossed the Deerfield River upstream. A drenching, lightning storm concealed their movements. Indian sentries at the ford mistook them for moose.

About half a mile from the falls, they dismounted. A few guarded the horses. The rest moved toward the camps. Waterfalls muffled their approach. At dawn, from a bluff, they looked down on the largest camp. Indians had taken shelter from the storm, feasted on beef cattle, then slept. No sentries, no dogs.

Colonists entered the first camp undetected. On signal, they fired into bark shelters, killing & wounding many. Those who dashed for the river were dispatched with gun or sword. Over a hundred Indians died. No captives, no exceptions.

Initially, the English lost one dead, a few wounded. They destroyed 2 forges for repairing guns, along with provisions & ammunition. Two great pigs of lead were thrown into the river. Meanwhile, warriors in adjacent Indian camps organized. One party positioned itself between the English & Deerfield. Another reached the tethered horses. Captain Turner fell, along with 36 others, including 13 from Northampton.

The Colonists recovered some mounts. Isaac Harrison permitted John Belcher to climb up behind him. After riding some distance, Harrison, wounded, fell part way off, then slipped to the ground. He said he'd like to rest awhile. Belcher rode on, heedless of Harrison's pleas.

Retreat became rout. Sixteen-year old Jonathan Wells, wounded in the leg, wandered alone in the woods for two days. Once he saved himself by hiding in a brush pile. Most survivors reached Hatfield that same day. A few took three days.

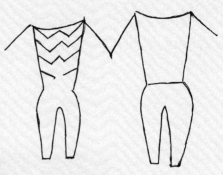

Woodland Indians, 1630-1680, inlaid pipes & clubs with scraps of broken trade kettles. Here two inlays form stick figures, their hands joined. Precisely such images occur in a widespread, iconographic systems depicting genealogy.[2] During the 17th & 18th centuries, Woodland Indians converted this system to war exploits, boasting of engagements, kills, captures. Details included sex of victims, weapons they held, etc. Examples were carved on clubs & trees, at least as early as 1642.[3]

A French document, dated 1666, explains this pictographic system. (A Seneca delegation was then in Paris.[4]) It shows inverted, headless human figures, presumably dead; captives led away; clan emblems (wolf, bear, turtle, etc.); tattoos & much more. It explains to the French this pictographic system. That system was familiar to Woodland tribes from New England to Ohio & surely must have been known to Colonists on the frontier.

1666

King Philip War

The snapping turtle, alone among turtles & tortoises in the Northeast, has a plastron with this shape. The Seneca emphasized this 'star' by painting it in colors sacred to them.[5] A star symbol alone might indicate turtle affiliation.

A thin 'spirit-line' connects the turtle's mouth (or soul) to the mouth of a human face, carved on the opposite side. I assume this face represents the club's owner, a turtle clan member or some personal identification. Painted below the face, like a tattoo, is a thunderbird. Among Woodland tribes, opposed bird & turtle represented Upper & Lower Worlds.

Above & below the face runs a central ridge. This ends in a raised, nucleated circle. A similar circle occurs on the opposite side. Other Woodland clubs have such lines, sometimes wavy, beginning or ending in circles. They may have symbolized power sources.

Depressions along the concave edge of the club once contained wampum. Each inlay represented a spinal vertebra. Many Woodland clubs, especially ball-headed clubs, were conceived as anthropomorphic, some explicitly so.

It's a curious club, more symbolic than functional. The grip resembles a European sword. Its grip's finial depicts an open-mouthed creature, probably an Underwater Panther. If so, it is an appropriate symbol. In Woodland cosmology, death swallows victims.

Did John King pick up this club in the Falls Fight? We know he was there.[6] I suspect, however, it came by another route. In this iconographic system, clubs were deliberately left behind as boasts & insults. It was even specified that a club's head should point in the direction from which its owner came.

Surely John King was pre-occupied during the Falls Fight, hardly in a souvenir-collecting mood. Moreover, this club was no weapon & weapons were used in the Falls Fight. It was largely symbolic, designed as such & abandoned as boast & insult. I think King came by this club after visiting the smoking ruins of a successful Indian raid.

MAI

A descendant of John King placed this club on loan to the MAI. She provided detailed family records. Someone discarded them. No loan record was prepared. The likely reasons for this can be inferred from the chapter on Deaccessioning. The club is now privately owned. Its alleged price: over $400,000.

CHAPTER 6   Problems

1928

James Ford & Harmon Hendricks died within 36 hours of one another. Ford was 84, Hendricks 82. Within months, Walter Warrell & William Harmon followed. The next year, Minor Keith was gone. Whatever Heye's dream may have been, it ended.

Ford's father founded U. S. Rubber. There was a brother, but he died. Ford inherited $22m. Hendricks came from a family known as the 'Kings of Copper.' He was the last family member to operate this business. Both were bachelors. Heye counted on $30m for his museum. Both chose kin, however distant. Ford left the MAI $50,000; Hendricks, $250,000; Warrell & Harmon, nothing; Keith, specimens.

Heye had always depended on others, starting with his mother. He, himself, contributed little. He paid off his $400,000 pledge in annual installments of $20,000, a fraction of the yearly budget. Now, he used $160,000 from Hendricks' will to complete his last eight payments. Forced to choose between an Edwardian life-style & his museum, there was never a choice.

Heye's solution: close the Museum. Thea talked him out of it. Let the museum support itself. Sell to operate. That's exactly what happened.

Legally, the beneficiaries of that collection were the People of the State of New York. Heye was its guardian. Even if he had been its principal benefactor — which he wasn't — the collection was still publicly owned. Donors qualified for tax relief. The museum paid no taxes. The moment the public enters, private property gets redefined.

When Heye chose not to maintain the museum, he was obliged to notify the State Attorney General. A court would have transferred it to another museum, probably the AMNH. Heye did no such thing. He knew this collection was a public trust. In 1915, when he moved his collection out of the University Museum, George Gordon asked for compensation. The collection, Heye said, no longer belonged to him, but to the newly created Museum of the American Indian.[1]

In 1935, negotiating with the Hidatsa tribe, Heye again defined that collection's legal status. To Daniel Wolf, a Waterbuster member, he wrote: 'The Board of Trustees derive their powers solely from the terms of the Foundation Deed under which this In-

84

stitution was founded and under the terms of which they hold all the specimens in the Museum. They have no authority to surrender them except in accordance with the law. The primary object of the Museum is to preserve and to keep safely for future generations anything pertaining to the life and history of the American Indians in a dignified and safe place where the descendants of the old Indians, as well as students and the public, can see and study the objects of veneration, beauty and historical or scientific interest that belonged to the Indians of the Americas. I am grateful that I have been instrumental in founding and fostering an institution of such size and dignity devoted exclusively to the preservation and the safe keeping of Indian relics so that they and their history will be available to future generations.'[2]

Perfectly stated. Yet, from 1928 to 1957, Heye sold specimens to finance Operations. His successor, Frederick Dockstader, did the same. These weren't arrowheads. Dealers chose the best. Collections were broken up, specimens scattered, records falsified.

1 9 2 9

The Depression didn't help. But, for this museum, it was already over. It ended when the MAI failed to inherit the $30m Heye expected from Ford & Hendricks.

'In 1929', Turbyfill ruminated, 'there was the crash. In one day, Heye lost this ROOM full of money. He called me down to his apartment at 912 Fifth Avenue and said, "Turbyfill, we're sunk. I've got to let everyone else go and you can't possibly do all that work alone."

'I said to him, "Mr. Heye, I'm surprised to hear you use the word 'cain't'." I had to talk two hours until I had him straightened out. . . . After that, everybody scattered.'[3]

1 9 3 0

The first Mrs. Heye died in 1924. According to Turbyfill, Heye turned his children over to boarding schools & summer camps: 'The girl, Mildred, worried about putting on weight like her daddy, traveled around and died in 1941. Larry, the boy, pitched ball at Dartmouth. He flunked out and came to New York to talk to his daddy.

'Heye phoned me and said, "Turbyfill, I'm sending my boy over to you to work for you every day from nine to five. I want you to see what he's made of and let me know."

'That didn't set very good with me. I thought, what a way to bring up a boy, where you have to ask somebody else to find out what he's made of.

'The boy come out — a great big old boy, six-one and weighing 190, and they don't come any nicer; but scared stiff of his daddy. He looks around and says, "I didn't know Dad had this place", and goes to work. He worked hard for me and was scared even to ask his daddy for lunch money. I told him, "Larry, if I had been you, I would have long ago flown the coop and got myself some overhauls and dug ditches."

'Heye sent him off somewhere else after a while, but Larry came back to Thanksgiving dinner with us, having no other place else. One day Heye took me aside and asked me what I thought of his son. Heye could always look me straight in the eye, but I could look him straighter than he could look me. I told him, "You ought to be proud of that boy."

'The boy got killed in an auto accident in 1932, at Ten Sleep, Wyoming, where he found a job as a ranch hand. He was twenty-two, the same age as Heye was when he first went west. I wondered, if that had been my boy, what would I have thought then.'[4]

1931

According to Burnett, George C. Fraser, an attorney, 'got into a rather sharp hassle with George Heye in 1931 and left the Board of Trustees somewhat abruptly.' Heye exercised an undated resignation he required before joining the Board.

Hendricks' will left a publication fund for the Hawikuh excavation, Arizona. It amounted to about $8000. Heye used it for maintenance, in Burnett's words, 'much to the consternation and disgust of Fred Hodge.' Fraser raised this matter at a Board meeting. 'Well', continued Burnett, 'those of us who knew George Heye can well understand how he felt about such interference.'[5]

Fraser had a point. A clear distinction was made between permanent endowment; gifts assigned to designated purposes (publication, building, etc); & unrestricted gifts which could be expended in full for operations. A Permanent Endowment Fund, started in 1918 with Thea Heye's gift of $550 in Liberty Bonds & an unstated sum from Frederick Hodge, was increased by a grant from the Hendricks estate for $250,000. Yet Heye treated restricted funds as unrestricted gifts.

Frederick Hodge became Director, Southwest Museum, Los Angeles. To finance his *History of Hawikuh*, anthropologists contributed what they could. Heye, perhaps out of embarrassment, contributed $3000. Some years later, when Dr. Hodge was ready to bring out the full report, Heye offered to finance it. Hodge felt, understandably, that the publication should be done under his supervision. It appeared long after all the principals were dead, under other names.[6]

Thea Heye was elected to the Board, 1933. Two years later, she died, comparatively young. Heye dismantled his Fifth Avenue apartment & took quarters at the University Club. He spoke of loneliness. He was, according to Mason, 'accustomed to a home with a hostess to dispense the amenities of gracious living.'[7] He couldn't stand club life. A year later, he married his third wife, Jessica Peebles Standing, of California.[8] She visited the Annex once.

Turbyfill: 'Heye brought her here one day to show her the place, as a kind of surprise, I guess. But she said she couldn't get out of the car because she had a cramp in her foot. I told her, "Pull off your shoes and walk around on my cold floor a little and it'll ease right up." It did, and she looked around, and I never heard of her afterwards.'[9] Divorce soon terminated the arrangement. Heye moved into the Ritz Tower.

BUDGET PROBLEMS

Thomas Roberts was the Museum's financial officer. According to Burnett, none of his arguments 'ever penetrated deeper into [Heye's brain] than the outer surfaces of his aural tympana [sic].' This used to infuriate Tom. Heye would go blithely off to the West Coast, or to Alaska, or to Europe, and leave Roberts holding the bag, the financial bag, of the Museum. I know that, on several occasions, Tom used, or rather, advanced from his own personal funds monies to meet the payrolls and, in a much smaller way, I, myself, from very meager funds, advanced monies to get shipments from off the wharf or out of a freight car.

'Roberts and Seward [Frederick Kimber Seward, trustee] occasionally got together with their common woes. At times, they would have me come downtown for luncheon so that museum matters might be discussed. Kim Seward had a keen sense of humor and he knew very well that I had much more insight into what George Heye was doing than I would admit to either of them. He used to look at me through those glasses of his, with their black ribbon, shake his head and say, "Ken, George Heye commits a felony and you compound it." And the only thing I could say to him was, "Oh, now listen, Kim, none of that legal stuff, please, I'm just an ordinary layman."

'I remember one particular day at luncheon, when the argument got pretty furious as to Museum expenditures as far as collections were concerned, and I said to Roberts, "No museum can exist that does not add to its collections. The moment that sort of thing stops, the institution dies." Kim Seward pushed his chair back and he said in that deep voice, "My God, Tom, we can't let that happen. There's no money to bury the damn place."'[10]

87

Junius Bird compared beginning & end: '[Heye] collected the best anthropologists, as well as the best artifacts. His place was a dream-come-true. His crew had money to dig up and buy everything the rest of us couldn't afford, during those years when it was still there to be got. They had the beginnings of a topnotch publishing program. They had the euphoria of believing they had lifetime tenure. They arranged for Heye to pick their brains and eventually were rewarded with the satisfaction of having their boss know quite a good deal.

'Heye was not an ungifted student. He remembered detail. He was such a compulsive that he had to write the catalog number, in his own hand, on every damned thing he bought. This made him the only museum patron on earth who knew what he had. Of course, if he decided this was a 3000-year-old Patagonian rock crystal ceremonial smoking bowl, it was.

'Heye had uneducable spots, though. He never could work up anything but boredom for potsherds — valuable in research the way fragments of dinosaur skeletons are valuable, for reconstruction purposes. Very often — though not always — he would welcome one of his archeologists home from a dig, gratefully relieve him of the artifacts he had bought, and tell him to forget about the careful tracings and notes that made the artifacts intelligible. One of the museum's unadvertised tasks at the moment is calling in such documentations from archeologists who got this treatment from Heye, a kind of treatment that caused a scandal Heye didn't understand.'[11]

Bird experienced this treatment firsthand. After Heye died, Bird delivered a second set of his notes on arctic excavations to the MAI. To date, these have not been found. Fortunately, Bird kept a set in his papers at the AMNH. Written across the top, in his hand: *Copy of Complete Set of Field-Notes pertaining to the 1928 Greenland Fieldwork. Originals presented to George Heye as documentation to accompany the collection placed in the Museum of the American Indian. As I have no faith in Heye preserving the original notes I am placing this copy in my papers.*'[12]

OBITUARY

In Heye's obituary, Lothrop wrote: [His] 'story is not entirely one of success, for he was a strong willed character who liked to do things his own way and did not make full use of the technical help he had assembled. For the guidance of future students, we should point out that the museum catalog, of which Heye personally took entire charge for most of his active life, is not what it should be.

88

'For this there are several reasons. In the first place, no field catalog numbers were entered into the Museum catalog and a great deal of information has been lost. On the other hand, Heye, if requested, personally added the Museum catalog numbers to the field catalog. Some of these double entries still exist in private hands.

'In the second place, nothing is entered in the catalog as "provenience unknown." Saville and the present writer were once shown a small statue of unrecorded type, acquired in a mixed collection without data, and were asked where it came from. One of us guessed Guatemala, the other Venezuela. I do not know which Heye chose, but a guess was recorded as fact.

'Heye', continued Lothrop, 'had no interest in potsherds — once they were catalogued and added to the count of the specimens in the Museum. When the Museum storage was moved to the Bronx, over 70 barrels of sherds were thrown away. So far as is known, there is no record of what was discarded. Some of these sherds came from stratified cuts which had not been published.

'George Heye led a complicated personal life, with which we are not concerned. His treatment of some of those who had served him loyally and well is still recalled and resented. On the other hand, others will remember his hospitality, generosity, and understanding.'[13]

POLICY

In the fall of 1917, Frederick Hodge arrived back in New York, after his first season excavating Hawikuh. 'I was utterly amazed, dumbfounded, to find … pottery fragments … all piled on the back of this table and the fellow who got through first, picked up a bag … with a totally different number… That was devastating … field numbers … were a vital part of this whole business…. Heye was acquisitive…. Specimens were his great object in life. Information respecting them didn't concern him.'[14]

Heye's evasive cataloging, ambivalence about documentation, anti-professionalism, Robber Baron bargaining, enigmatic idiosyncrasies, were alleged & true, overwhelmingly.

The *MAI Annual Report*, 1971:14, states:

> A continuing project was started at our Research Branch which involves the reviewing of the North American archaeological collections to relieve the storage area of useless artifacts.
>
> Curator William F. Stiles

18th Century Club

18TH CENTURY CLUB (15/4230)

Travelers to colonial America often returned with Indian trophies, especially war clubs & moccasins. Some were commissioned for natural history cabinets. Indian seamstresses even tailored local costumes for visitors. Back home, they posed for portraits with a forest background.

Most trophies were simply souvenirs, sometimes made by traditional methods, but nevertheless, souvenirs. Those placed in curio cabinets or linen closets often remained in mint condition, having never been used.

SIR WILLIAM JOHNSON (1715-1774)

A fair number reached England via Sir William Johnson. As Superintendent of Indian Affairs for the Northern District, he occupied an ideal position to collect. A network of agents searched for old pieces. They commissioned some, acquired a few old ones, whatever. Johnson's private collection became one of the minor wonders of colonial America.[1]

Correspondents begged for examples. Demand exceeded supply. Two hundred years of trade turned New England tribes into European consumers. Johnson looked westward. By the 1760s, the local supply was minimal. Johnson imported from as far west as the Eastern Plains.[2]

Romantics wanted Indians to look Indian. On special occasions, some did. When representatives of the Six Nations entered Albany, August 8, 1746, Mohawks appeared in full panoply. At their head marched their new war-captain, William Johnson, 'dressed, painted and plumed as required by the dignity of his rank.'[3]

Johnson enjoyed a good press. The artist, Benjamin West, helped. One engraving, based on a West drawing, shows Indians delivering English captives. A babe, arms outstretched, rushes to a British officer, while a second clings to its adopted Indian mother. Unmentioned was the fact that these were property exchanges. The receiver could sell his new property into bondage or, if shipped to the Caribbean, into slavery.[4]

JOHNSON HALL

On May 22, 1776, Capt. Joseph Bloomfield, Third New Jersey Regiment, entered Johnson Hall. This fort-like, pseudo-stone structure originally served as Johnson's home & headquarters. But Sir William had died two years earlier. Johnson Hall was now the home of his son, Sir John. Lady Mary was pregnant.

Bloomfield came to evict her. He tells how he wandered through rooms filled with wampum belts, costumes, powder horns, smoking pipes & other artifacts, scattered among portraits, prints, coats of arms, weapons. A full description, he wrote, 'would exceed the bounds of my Journal.'[5]

That collection became a casualty of war. First, it was looted by officers of the Third New Jersey Regiment. General George Washington followed this court martial with interest.[6] The Johnson collection was scattered at auctions. Governor George Clinton acquired several pieces for Pierre du Simitiere, a Philadelphia artist, antiquary, naturalist. Such pieces, Clinton wrote, 'tho well worth preserving, are wantonly scattered abroad, many of them lost, & others at the Hands of Clowns who know not their Value.'[7]

When Du Simitiere died, his collection went to other collectors, including Charles Wilson Peale, who established his own museum in Philadelphia.

THE CLUB

Club 15/4230 is a traditional ball-headed war club with iron spike. The crest bears the likeness of an Underwater Panther. Such clubs were conceived as anthropomorphic. The ball, representing a human head, is about to be swallowed by a mythic panther. In Woodland cosmology, Death swallows victims, consigning them 'from sunshine to a sunless land.'

1666

A 1666 French document (opposite) is entitled: 'Portrait of a Savage on a board in their cabin on which they ordinarily paint how often he has been to war, how many men he has taken and killed.'[8] It's generally attributed to the Seneca, for a delegation of Seneca was then in Paris. Reproduced imperfectly in O'Callaghan.[9] Dr. William Sturtevant corrected the portrait & translated the text.[10]

The most striking feature is the portrait, 'A', recognizable for its tattoos (*les piqures*). One of these tattoos is the 'star' icon representing a turtle affiliation. The remaining tattoos, all presumably ancient, were certainly familiar to 17th-18th century Woodland warriors.

In 'B' we see two 'mats.' Each represents a battle or raid. The two mats are connected, for 'he did not return to his village, but returned with other parties whom he met or formed', in other words, a second raid. In 'C' the broken arrow 'denotes that they were wounded on this expedition.' 'D' connotes two 'belts [offered with outstretched arms] to raise a war party and to avenge the death of . . . someone belonging to them or . . . the same tribe.' In 'E', the broken arrow again represents wounding. The line connecting these belts indicates 'he has gone back to fight without having entered his village.'

To the left of this sequence, we see stick-figure captives joining hands. Each holds a weapon. 'F & F' represent 'two men taken prisoner': one with musket, the other with hatchet. 'G' represents a 'woman, distinguished from [a] man by a kind of waistcloth.' 'H' represents 'a man whom he killed in battle, who had a bow and arrows.'

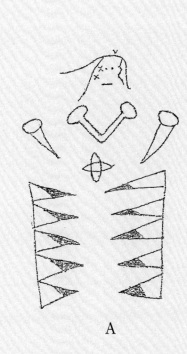

A

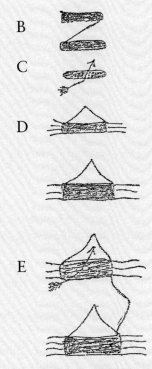

B

C

D

E

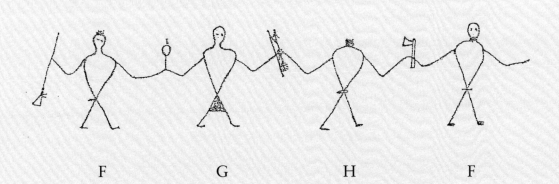

F   G   H   F

One side of the handle shows 13 human figures, each with traditional hourglass or X body, joined by their hands. Each holds a musket.

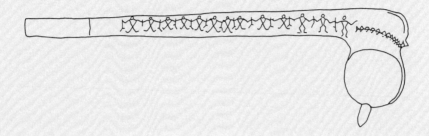

The opposite side offers a classic example of exploit iconography. The engraver, in shorthand, recorded successive exploits: engagements, kills, captures, wounds, losses.

On the back handle, at the top, appears a human figure closely resembling the 'Portrait' on the 'Board' painting, 'A'. It should not surprise us. These were traditional tattoos.

Below this appears an inscription in Onondaga & French, rendered in lower case Latin letters: oq8entaquete le camarade jeanson.[11] It's been interpreted as referring to Otqueandageghte ('He bears a belly'), an Onondaga warrior, presumably the club's owner. The added French words identify Otqueandagehte as Johnson's comrade.

Otqueandageghte learned French while living with Indians at Oswegatchie or La Presentation (Ogdenburg). Johnson weaned him away from this allegiance. They became friends.

The underside of the handle bears an inscription in upper case Latin letters. These are less worn, presumably by a later hand: WATKONOCHROCHQUANYO WARRAGHIYAGEY. Both phrases are Iroquoian. The first translates: 'I greet you as a relative' or 'I esteem you very much.' The second is Johnson's name, given to him by the Mohawk, 1746.

Alexander Farquharson, an 18th century British officer & collector of 'Savage Curiositys', said the name meant 'a tall and stately tree, with wide spreading branches.'[12] Other translations are equally suspect. More likely, if tradition was followed, the adopted name came from a deceased Mohawk war chief. About a dozen different spellings exist. J.N.B. Hewitt, native speaker & gifted ethnologist, found all untranslatable.[13] Johnson spelled it exactly as it appears on the club.

English outposts often had soldiers gifted in engraving. Perhaps Johnson hired one to add his name. Like the wampum belts in Johnson Hall, the club documented an alliance. That alliance didn't last. Otqueandageghte fought with the French against the British at the German Flats, 1758. At first he was thought to have died there, for a weapon bearing the above inscriptions was found among the dead.[14]

Leaving a club on a battlefield was a standard boast. Otqueandagehte made this defiant statement in traditional manner. He lived on: changing sides, moving about, spying, creating mischief.[15] In 1773, chiefs at Caughnawaga complained that his appointment as a chief, by the British, lacked their approval. They dismissed him as one who had 'no certain place of abode.'[16]

Peter Wraxall, Sir William Johnson's private secretary, recorded this weapon as knife, not club. Yet none of the inscriptions would fit on a knife handle. Presumably Wraxall learned of this second hand & mistook the club for a knife.[17]

LOUIS SCHELLBACH

In 1928, Louis Schellbach, on Heye's staff, published an account of this club.[18] He suggested it reached England via Sir William's son, John. Sir John had other problems. In May 1776, he hurriedly departed Johnson Hall with 170 Scottish tenants & friends & went over the Adirondacks to Akwesasne. There he raised a small army of Canadiennes & Indians. In July, they marched to relieve Montreal, but arrived 2-3 hours after a British regiment re-occupied the town.[19]

A contemporary account tells of Sir John emerging from the forest at the head of his party of Loyalists, complete with brass 6-pounder. The Indians, 'about 100 very fine men', were highly painted. The Whites wore ordinary clothes, save Sir John who, in buckskin, carried a tomahawk, wore a scalping knife on his chest & a hat encircled with a snakeskin, its rattle in front.[20]

Did Sir John pack & ship Otqueandageghte's war club, as Schellbach suggested? More likely it went earlier, sent by Sir William who had reason not to keep it.

ROBERT ABELS

In 1927, a young American arms dealer, Robert Abels, saw the club in England, 'bundled with South Pacific clubs.' He sold it to Heye for $25. The next year, when the Museum published Schellbach's account, Abels accused Heye of concealing its true value, deception, dishonesty, much more. He demanded $1000.

Heye asked Charles A. Adams, Director of the New York State Museum, for an evaluation. Adams consulted a curator, Arthur Parker, a Seneca. He also asked the opinion of A. C. Flick, then editing Sir William Johnson's papers. On their advice, Adams advised Heye, 1931, '$250.00 is none too much to pay.'[21]

Heye declined. Abels sued. Heye returned the club, along with a letter from Heye's counsel. At which point, Abels withdrew all charges, abjectly apologized, & thanked Heye for not asking him to return the $25.[22]

Decades later, Abels sold the club to a collector; bought it back; then sold it to James Economos for $25,000. In 1974, the Canadian Museum of Civilization acquired it for $35,000.

CHAPTER 7   # Repatriation

In the Beginning, there were two Thunderbirds. Each decided to be reincarnated as an Indian. One chose a Hidatsa virgin to be his mother. Since she belonged to the Midipati or Waterbuster Clan, that became his clan, appropriately so, for his special powers caused rain to fall & crops to grow. He became a great Hidatsa medicine man. When enemies attacked, his sacred pipe put them to flight. His medicine brought rain, grass, buffalo.

Toward the end of his life, he accepted an invitation to visit the other Thunderbird. His old friend had chosen to be reincarnated among the Shiwaliuwa, nomads to the south who followed the buffalo, camping in tents beside fresh streams & springs. Permanent homes, the Shiwaliuwa Thunderbird said, were filthy. He proposed that the Hidatsa's head become his keepsake. The Hidatsa proposed, instead, that his friend visit him. After that, he said, they could decide whose head became whose keepsake.

Back home, the Hidatsa commanded his wives to sweep the lodge & cool the floor with water. They prepared dishes of corn, squash & sunflower seeds. They added peppermint to water. He himself prepared the tobacco. On the appointed day, his wives, dressed in their finest, brought wood for the fire, but delayed lighting it. The Shiwaliuwa Thunderbird descended through the smoke hole, then sat in darkness. The fire, when lit, revealed him. He surveyed the lodge interior, then his friend's wives. Porridge of corn & beans was set before him. Other dishes followed. He tried them all, finishing with tobacco. At which point, he said he'd erred: his head should become the keepsake of his friend.

They agreed to a battle between their tribes. The Hidatsa would win, with the Shiwaliuwa Thunderbird last to fall. 'Hurry out then with your pipe and offer me a smoke.' When the pipe touched his lips, he died. His head was cut off, cleaned on an ant-hill & placed in a Hidatsa shrine.

The Hidatsa Thunderbird said, 'When I die, place my head beside the other & keep both sacred. Appoint custodians.' That happened. As to early custodians, I have no knowledge. But, being old, I remember one named [Missouri] River. When he died, Slim Shin was appointed.

'Both skulls were kept in a shrine. No one walked in front of them. Mice that passed at night lay dead in the morning. Only appointed custodians could expose those skulls & only in days of distress.

'Few warriors survived the smallpox of 1837. When the Sioux attacked, the skulls protected us. During my time, the Sioux attacked in great numbers. Sometimes we feared they would clean us up. But, when we placed those skulls on the housetop, lightning & thunder chased our enemies. I took part in those battles.

'Wherever the skulls were, the Waterbuster Clan kept the housetop clean. A visitor who went to that housetop died there.

'Custodians carried those skulls wherever we moved. At Fishhook Village, they placed them facing west, from where the rains came. Later they took them to a place called Independence. That was their last stand.'[1]

GILBERT L. WILSON (1868-1930)

In 1907, at Independence, North Dakota, the Rev. Gilbert L. Wilson, a Presbyterian missionary, purchased 29 Hidatsa specimens for George Heye. Among them was the shrine. It resembled a drying rack, with 4 posts, 2 platforms. The lower shelf held 2 human skulls, painted red, polished from handling & sealed in a painted parfleche container.

Beside this bundle lay a painted buffalo skull with eagle feathers attached to the horns; an eagle-wing fan; a box-turtle shell; & a hat left as an offering. Over the shrine, completely covering the skull bundle, were 2 buffalo robes; a trade blanket; & 70 yards of varied calico, again left as offerings.[2]

Adjoining the shrine stood a post from which hung a second bundle. This contained varied animal & human parts, wild turnips, small stones & an unsmoked medicine pipe. Together these represented eagle hunting, warfare & personal medicines.

Wilson collected for museums. He paid the Hidatsa $300.85 for these 29 specimens. Of this, $100 went to Wolf Chief for the shrine.[3] Wolf Chief wasn't a clan member, though his father, Small Ankle (d. 1888), had been & served as a keeper of that shrine. 'When a keeper got too old to care for the mysteries', Wolf Chief said, 'he sold it . . . to another [member of the clan] who gave rich gifts for the privilege.'[4]

At Small Ankle's death, no replacement stepped forward to buy the shrine. It remained in Small Ankle's earth lodge until his widow died in 1901. Then Wolf Chief transferred it to his own earth lodge, placing it in the equivalent space. Though a member of the Praire Chicken Clan, he became, by default, its reluctant guardian.

He asked eligible elders to care for it. All refused: 'Sam Jones and Scattered Village wanted nothing to do with the bundle; Foolish Bear's wife did not want it in her house; Butterfly said he traveled so much he would not be able to take proper care of it. Hairy Coat advised Wolf Chief to leave it alone until its earth lodge fell down around it, but others disagreed. Wolf Chief thought of burying it, but was told such an action would not be appropriate.'[5] The Indian agent had outlawed traditional ceremonies required of a keeper. Any who performed them risked jail.

Missionaries viewed sacred bundles as obstacles to conversion. Wolf Chief had converted. He no longer prayed to the old gods. But he wished them no ill. He still believed the shrine brought rain, buffalo, cured illness, granted victory in war.[6] He told of two skeptics who mocked its powers: lightning killed both.[7] He also told how, in 1866, when he was 17, drought threatened. People brought offerings to the shrine. Small Ankle sang & prayed. Rain followed. 'Some men . . . measured the earth: it was wet one foot.'[8]

Yet no eligible guardian stepped forward. For 18 years, Wolf Chief protected the shrine. Then, in 1906, Gilbert Wilson arrived. Previously, Wolf Chief hadn't let Whites see it. He feared 'the *spirits* might be made angry.' But, convinced of Wilson's sincerity, he let him see the shrine & let Wilson's brother, Frederick, sketch it.

NEGOTIATIONS

Wilson returned the next year, determined to buy the shrine, along with its attendant songs & stories. His diary entry for July 9, 1907, is ethnography at its best: 'A gentle rain was falling as we went into Wolf Chief's cabin. We found him sitting looking at the painting of the shrine which my brother made and which I had delivered but a day or two before. I began speaking thru Goodbird as interpreter.

'You will remember a year ago that I spoke about your selling the shrine and the medicine bag which is in the earth lodge. I tried to get the North Dakota Historical Society to buy them, but I failed. Then I tried in other places, for I did not want the shrine and its story to be lost. At last, only a week or two before I left Minneapolis, a man wrote me from New York. He is wealthy and interested in the Indians. He told me to buy the shrine if I could — so I came up to see you. If you will sell and will name a price, if it is within my means, I will buy it now; if not, then I will write to the man in New York and tell him what you want for the shrine and ask him if he wants to buy. The man's name is Mr. Heye. He is going to build a big house with fine floors and windows where Indian things can be kept and shown and where they can't be destroyed by fire or moths.

'Wolf Chief looked very grave.

'While all that Mr. Wilson says is true', he answered, addressing Goodbird, 'since I saw him last year, I have been changing my mind. While I believe in one God and pray to him, yet these things were my father's and I like to keep them in honor of him. I have thought I would maybe roof over the earth lodge again and make it strong and dry. . . .

'I can quite understand', I answered him, 'why you may wish to keep the things. But . . . you know that as late even as 50 years ago there were many white people who said it was of no use to try to teach the Indians anything, that the only good Indian was a dead Indian, and for us to pay out money to send schoolteachers among them would only be a waste of our means. . . .

'Then there arose some men who said, "Maybe the reason we haven't been able to civilize the Indian and get him to live in houses and plant farms is because we don't understand him. Let us send men who will make a study of his ways of living — find out what he thinks, how he elects his chiefs and how he looks on us. Perhaps the reason we are not able to make him understand us is because we do not understand him."

'So, for this reason, learned men formed the Ethnological Bureau, and sent students to the different Indian tribes to see what they could find. And everybody was astonished to find out how much more the Indian knew than we were aware and that his myths and beliefs and government and religion were all interesting.

'Now this is why I am out here working among you Indians. Mr. Heye is not a trader. He does not do these things for money and neither do I. All I get for my buying is about half my expenses of my month on the Reservation. But I want to buy the shrine for Mr. Heye so he can put it in a big fireproof house where it will be safe and where people can come and see it. And I want to get the story of the shrine and your picture and the story of your life and hang them up in a frame or else print them in a little book so that when white people see the shrine, they can read the story and know what it all means. Then, when their congressmen in Washington vote for money to send teachers among the Indians, they won't call him a fool, but will say, "That is the right thing to do. I have seen the shrine and read what it means and those Indians can think and tell real interesting stories. They are worth civilizing."'

'It was evident that Wolf Chief was impressed somewhat, but I was hardly prepared for the honest confession of old belief which followed. He spoke: "Well, maybe after all the *spirits* want to be taken to New York and be put into that big house where they will be kept nice and dry and not have to stay in the damp earth lodge. Perhaps it is the spirits which put it into Mr. Wilson's mind to come and ask to buy the shrine. Besides, everything that Mr. Wilson promised has come true. He promised us pictures and other things last year and everything he has said he would do he has done. . . . Then, too, I have not dreamed of my father for a long time until last night when I dreamed he came to me and told me I was going to get something today. Perhaps what I get is what Mr. Wilson will pay me."'

'I was hardly prepared to close the bargain without consulting Mr. Heye, but asked, "How much do you ask for them?"'

'I want a great deal of money. I want more than a hundred dollars! . . . But I want the money today. For if Mr. Wilson pays me today, I will think it is what my father wishes me to do. But if he does not, I will think I ought to keep the things.'

'That is right, Wolf Chief', I answered. 'But [Mr. Heye] . . . would not want me to [buy it] until I had seen the shrine and seen everything is in order for that is the way white people do business. But that won't take long. We can go down to the lodge in a few minutes and decide on the sale at once.'

'Meanwhile, the rain had increased and it was evident that Wolf Chief was uneasy about something: "What you say is true," he said, "and I believe now in one true God and pray to Him, who is over all spirits. But the shrine was used mostly to get rain and I have seen it come true many, many times. It is raining now. . . ."'

[I answered]: 'I am sure I can give no disrespect to anything if I go down to the lodge with no wish to mock at the things. . . . I don't think any harm will come if I go down to the lodge with the right motive.'

'This seemed to convince Wolf Chief, especially as the sun was now shining. We went down and, as among the offerings on the shrine were two prime buffalo robes, I closed at once, paying part down and the rest later in the evening. As I made final payment, Wolf Chief said: "I am glad to get so much money today and I am glad to have sold the shrine for another thing. These were my father's medicines and tho I believe in one true God and pray to Him, for I used to pray to these things and they did me no good, yet sometimes I get to thinking of old times and of these medicines. Perhaps now when they are gone, I will not think of them so much."'[9]

ORIN G. LIBBY (1864-1952)

Earlier Wilson had offered the shrine to the local Historical Commission. Its director, Orin G. Libby, wanted it — for free. Libby was furious when Heye bought it. The press quoted him as saying Wilson took the shrine illegally & escaped 'from the state before the other Indians of the [clan] could . . . prevent the loss of their most sacred possessions.' He asked that Wilson be barred from the reservation.[10]

The same Waterbuster elders who had earlier declined to guard the shrine, now denounced its sale. They said it had been taken illegally & now lay neglected among strangers. Their distress reached Washington. Wilson's permit to enter the reservation was suspended.

Wilson asked Heye to send Wolf Chief a photograph of the shrine, as displayed in the Museum. I found no evidence he did. I doubt if the shrine was ever displayed. Heye left it un-catalogued for over 30 years.

The bill of sale records $160 paid to Wolf Chief.[11] I assume the $60 difference covered the two robes. Considering the dollar's value, then & there, plus the limited market for Indian shrines, surely this was top offer, probably the only offer.

Money, not ownership, created resentment. If nature had destroyed the shrine, no one would have noticed. If it had been given to the Historical Society, no one would have protested. But, $160? That belonged to the Waterbuster Clan. The community watched. Misfortune soon beset Wolf Chief. Lightning nearly killed him. None of his many children survived him. His house & store burned. Still, '. . . my good peoples help me out', he wrote to Wilson. Neighbors re-equipped him. He prospered. By 1911, he advised Wilson, 'You can come on reservation again and we do the best we can for you', adding 'my medicines are stronger than Prof. Libby['s] medicine.'[12]

ALFRED W. BOWERS (1901-1990)

The record goes silent for 28 years. Then, in 1934, George Heye received a letter that began: 'I have in my office Drags Wolf, Bears Arms, Louie Wolf and Arthur Mandan of the Hidatsa Tribe.' The letter tells of severe drought. Clan elders blame this on the loss of their shrine. They offer $75 for its return. Signed: 'Alfred W. Bowers.'[13]

Today, repatriation claims are routine. In 1934 they were virtually unknown, certainly to George Heye. Repatriation seemed totally unrealistic. So much lost, so little saved. Museums seemed the only hope. Those who preserved were mostly Whites, out of private dedication, at personal expense. George Heye saw himself in those terms.

Bowers' demand stunned him. Heye offered no apology: 'I have never known of a "water buster bundle"... I never purchased any specimens from Wolf Chief. In 1907 I bought from the Reverend G. L. Wilson a Hidatsa shrine, which is no longer in my possession, but that of the Museum of the American Indian. I no longer have any personal control over the object.'[14]

A local missionary supported Heye: 'Just a few Indians are doing this', wrote the Rev. H. W. Case, 'spurred on by a white man ... one of the higher men of the Clan hopes this will not go thru ... if put to a petition, only a dozen would approve.... I ask that you keep my name out of this.'[15]

Bowers' next letter bore the thumb-prints & signatures of 13 Clan elders: 'The Water Buster Clan still survives, and there are a great number of us.... Mr. Wolf Chief's father, Small Ankle, was a member of the Clan and during his life, it was his duty to be the keeper of this Medicine which hung in the Medicine Lodge. But the bundle did not belong to [him] alone, but to the whole Clan.

'After Small Ankle's death, when Wolf Chief converted to Christianity, Mr. Wilson persuaded him to sell this sacred relic, telling him that otherwise he could not belong to the church.

'As no one but a Water Buster is supposed to care for or touch this sacred bundle, we feel that its loss is the cause of the many misfortunes visited upon our people.

'... we have not made a previous demand [because] Wolf Chief was the son of ... a Water Buster, therefore our son and we did not wish to humiliate and embarrass him during his life time. Mr. Wolf Chief is now dead.

'Indian relics obtained in this manner is an insult to the Indian and surely a disgraceful slur upon the white man's tactics.'[16]

Though signed by 13 elders, Bowers wrote this letter. He conceived the demand, handled the paperwork, generated publicity. He wasn't the first to advocate repatriation, but he was the first to recruit the media. In this, he was 50 years ahead of his time.

Outsiders, at least in the past, usually initiated repatriation claims. It could hardly be otherwise. Conquest proved so destructive, resistance stood no chance. In parts of America, you need a shovel to prove Indians ever lived there. George Heye knew all this. Yet he couldn't imagine what possessed Bowers. He asked locals to check him out.

COLLIER VS. CHASE

Bowers recruited John Collier (1884-1968), famed Commissioner of Indian Affairs. Collier, a diplomat of great charm, asked the Museum Board to 'give sympathetic consideration to this request.'[17] Heye promised to 'put the entire matter before [the Board].'[18]

Five more letters from the Rev. Case advised Heye to stall: '. . . [Bowers] bluffing . . . pushing it . . . one Clan elder said, "Tell Mr. Heye the bundle is where it ought to be and *Must Not Come Back*" . . . Bowers not to be trusted. . . . Two thirds of the signers didn't realize what they were signing. . . .

'[Bowers] said your Museum was on the rocks financially . . . all these things would be lost . . . tried to work the Indians up into making him Supt of the Reservation . . . showed ignorance if he thought Indian power could put him in . . . the Supt's job is a civil service one . . . has few friends with the Indians . . . [no] more than eight or ten are pushing this bundle affair.'[19]

That March, Heye wrote to John Collier: 'I have devoted the better part of my life and practically all of my fortune to the building up of [this] Institution. . . . Our museum is dignifiedly and appropriately housed and contains unduplicatable collections readily available to the student and open without cost to the public. Insofar as the Indians of these times are concerned, it was my intention, which I think I have successfully carried out, to found an institution where the objects which had been sacred to them, but which were falling into disuse and in danger of destruction under modern conditions, could be preserved and given proper and understanding treatment in sympathetic surroundings.

'In all my personal experience with North American Indians, I never had any question like this raised before and I am at a loss to understand the present request in view of the invariable record of friendliness of Indians everywhere to this institution.'[20]

The Rev. Case was delighted: '. . . beautifully settled.' Heye realized this settled nothing. He sent Case travel funds to collect statements from clan elders who opposed returning the shrine. Case warned that a delegation might soon visit Washington: 'they still think they can get the shrine.'[21]

The delegation did visit Washington, then New York. Heye remained unmoved. In February, 1937, his Board unanimously declined to return the shrine.

The Reservation superintendent earlier reported to Collier that he 'found no fraud or misrepresentation . . . return of these medicine bundles will depend entirely upon the good will of the Heye Foundation.'[22] Collier forwarded this to Heye, with a postscript: '. . . if the Museum should make a GIFT of the bundles back to the tribe, and proper publicity were given, the result in Indian good-will in many tribes would be a gratifying and valuable one.'[23]

HEYE SKEPTICAL

Heye solicited further information about Bowers. The Indian Office assured him of Bowers' sincerity. 'The Indians, in general, feel friendly toward him.'[24] Bowers was no stranger to them. They'd known him since he was six, when his parents homesteaded land adjoining the Reservation. He taught in rural schools, saved, then attended Beloit College. Beloit was one of the few colleges in America with both an anthropology program & museum. Graduate work at Chicago followed, then research among the Mandan of North Dakota. The Mandan adopted him as 'Four Bears', the name of their greatest leader.

In 1932, Bowers obtained a small grant to continue his Hidatsa studies: 'I am settled conveniently here . . . in the agency village. The hotel has four rooms and two guests. We get meals at 20 cents and room for $10 a month which is cheaper than I could feed myself. I need to take my lunch out when working, which is extra. . . . I have been working on the Thunderbird bundle since last week, taking down the myth in the Hidatsa language.'[25]

When the grant ended, he returned to his farm. A renter's family occupied the house. He moved into a granary.[26] Later, as a clerk with the Drought Agency, he continued his studies & pressed for the return of the shrine. Recruiting Collier proved decisive. Heye finally yielded. From Washington came praise: 'rejoicing . . . gratifying . . . generous.'

Rumors of this reached the Rev. Case: 'I would not like to see it go thru . . . Mandan [one of the applicants] is a good-for-nothing . . . not the will of the people but only a few urged on by Mr. Collier. . . . My main interest is that they do not make liars out of Wolf Chief or Wilson.'[27]

But it did 'go thru.' On Dec. 3, 1937, the MAI Board unanimously voted to exchange the shrine 'for some article authoritatively antique or valuable. . . . [This] is in no way a recognition on our part of any legal or moral obligation to return the Bundle to the Clan', but is done solely to cement 'the cordial relationships which have always existed between our Museum and the various Indian Tribes.

'Sympathetic as we are with the desire of the Indians to perpetuate their own culture and traditions, we are glad to find a way to help them which we feel is within the limits of our authority as Trustees.'[28]

In exchange, the Hidatsa offered a horn & club, both sacred. They further agreed, should the shrine ever again leave the tribe, it would 'automatically return to the Heye Foundation.' Forty-five Waterbusters signed this contract.[29]

MEDIA EVENT

Drags Wolf, 79, Foolish Bear, 84, each in full regalia, with Mandan as interpreter, took a train east. Photographers & reporters covered every stop. America listened by radio & watched by newsreel. In New York, four delegates from Washington waited.

On Jan. 14, 1938, CBS, NBC & Movienews covered this event. A crowd filled Audubon Terrace. Inside, dignitaries surrounded a polished table. Drags Wolf & Foolish Bear presented the horn & club, recounting the history of each, at length. Heye then handed them the skulls, exposed. Consternation!

Only appointed guardians could touch the Thunderbirds. Drags Wolf & Foolish Bear instantly resolved the problem. They re-named Heye '*Isatsigibis*', Slim Shin, after an earlier guardian. Then the three smoked a pipe.[30]

The following spring, rains drenched the Dakotas.[31] Heye loved this part of the story. What he never mentioned was that he kept the pipe, fan, two robes & shrine. Had the shrine been catalogued when acquired, 1907, its number would have been 1/3801. Instead, Heye assigned it 7/8199, a 1918 number. Even that is suspect. The NMAI has duplicate catalogs, each with about 246,000 cards. All are machine-numbered, except for a few. Two of those are numbered 7/8199. The paper differs. Heye hand numbered both. In other words, he went to that effort to deceive.

In the 1980s, the Inventory staff discovered the pipe & fan. They returned these to the Hidatsa. The robes couldn't be found. The shrine lay 'in pieces.' I don't know its fate.

But I do know the fate of the rivals Wilson, Libby & Bowers. All took higher degrees in anthropology. Libby's temper worked against him, but he did good work. Bowers published authoritative accounts of Hidatsa ethnology. And Wilson, well, he proved to be special.

He arrived as a missionary so uptight, he recorded pregnancy beliefs in Latin. By the time he died in 1930, he was a surrogate Hidatsa elder. Robert Lowie, veteran ethnologist, met him in 1910: 'Among the Hidatsa, I was taken down another peg. The Reverend Gilbert L. Wilson was neither particularly cultivated nor in any sense intellectual, but he was a superb observer. In the recording of ethnographic detail — about house building or pottery making or farming customs or the care of infants, for example — I, the trained ethnologist, could not begin to compete with him.'[32]

As Wilson saw it, the conventional ethnologist 'takes up a special subject, say the corn dance. He asks: "What were its special features, What things in it are to be emphasized, etc. . . . The proper and essential way, in my mind . . . is to take a typical and intelligent informant and . . . [get] from him your major account, out of his own experiences. Then follow with corroborative accounts, also from personal experience, preferably from other members of the same family. Then add corroborative evidences from any other source.'[33]

Claude Lévi-Strauss called Wilson's study of Hidatsa eagle trapping 'one of the finest masterpieces in all anthropological literature. . . . [He] had the inspired idea of allowing his informants to talk freely, and of respecting the harmonious and spontaneous infusion, in their stories, of anecdote and meditation, humble technological actions and intricate liturgical ritual; of hunting, cooking and fishing, on the one hand, and rites and rituals on the other.'[34]

Masterwork

Heye purchased this mask in 1914 from W. O. Oldman, a London dealer. I imagine it reached England via a Northwest Coast trader, perhaps as early as the late 18th century. No detail of its provenience survives, though we recognize it as the work of a Tsimshian carver. It was displayed in a case prominently labeled: 'Masterworks of Northwest Coast Art.'

JUNE, 1982: five pieces from that case, including this mask, disappeared. I read press accounts. It was mentioned on TV. About a week later, I phoned Roland Force, then the museum director. The police, he said, had no leads. I offered to make inquiries. He urged me to do so. I called a dealer I respected.

'You waited too long,' he said. 'Last week they could be had for $10,000. Now they've changed hands at least once.' He promised to inquire. I checked my watch. He called back in 4 1/2 minutes: '$50,000.'[1]

I called Force. He proposed that an insurance investigator, William Smith, handle the matter. The museum's policy didn't cover Smith's services. Would I? Yes.

The missing pieces had a market value of over a million. But — stolen, easily recognized —. I assumed they'd been taken for ransom. Ransoming art involves three players: police, insurers, informers. Informers are generally the thieves. Police use them for bigger bait. Insurers pay informers. A three-way game. The danger: uninsured objects may be destroyed. These pieces were not insured.

JULY 21: Robert Venables, Curator of Education, learned (in confidence), that a local gallery owner, Christopher Selser, wrote to the police anonymously, saying the missing pieces were being peddled, gallery to gallery, by Emanuel Marin (alias Fernandez), a textile restorer at the Pillowry Shop. Smith checked: yes, the police had Selser's letter, actually several letters from different galleries. All named Marin. The police knew him well. He'd long served them as an informer, following a single conviction, decades earlier. In exchange for tips, the police overlooked his capers. They did so here.

AUGUST 11: Selser reported Marin wanted $10,000, plus immunity. Smith recommended against it. Force flew to Hawaii. In the meantime, Marin left four pieces with Selser, keeping the fifth as 'security' for the $10,000.

AUGUST 30: The museum staff learned of a forthcoming press account. They feared Marin might destroy the remaining piece. From Hawaii, Force instructed Venables: 1/ pick up $10,000 cash at a bank & deliver it to Selser; 2/ Selser to leave the gallery to retrieve the fifth piece; 3/ no police action until all pieces recovered.

What Force didn't tell Venables was that the museum's new Assistant Director, George Eager, would accompany him, as would William Smith, the insurance investigator.[2] Eager was to tape-record conversations secretly & Smith to go wired to the meeting with Selser.

AUGUST 31: Venables planned to take the subway to the bank, then a cab to the gallery. Instead, a chauffeured limo appeared. Venables, Eager & Smith climbed in. The recorded conversation survives: no one trusted anyone else. 'Don't point your finger at me!' 'You just did it to me!' Only the driver remained calm. He turned out to be a city detective.

They picked up the cash & went to the gallery. Smith followed Venables in. Police outside monitored conversations inside the gallery. Venables & Selser exchanged prepared receipts for specimens & cash. Then, with Eager's help, they started to carry the four pieces to the limo. Undercover police forced them back into the gallery. Venables was frisked — hands on wall, legs spread. At the 19th Precinct, he was arrested, but not booked.

The police staged an encounter between Venables & Marin. Neither recognized the other. Venables then produced a notarized document, on MAI stationary, authorizing his role. The desk sergeant gave him a receipt for the $10,000 & released him, six hours later.

Marin arranged for the missing mask to be delivered to the police. He spent the night in jail. The next morning, his lawyer, a former criminal court judge, appeared. The two walked out together. No charges were pressed.

George Eager, whose uncle was an editor at *The New York Times*, arranged for a news item favoring Roland Force's conspiracy theory.[3] Selser, with a friend at the *New York Post*, fared better: HERO HELPS COPS RECOVER $1M INDIAN ART.[4]

Force suspected Venables of theft & Selser of collusion. Yet they alone acted responsibly. Venables lost his job at the MAI & found no academic employment for six years. He's now at Cornell University. Selser closed his New York gallery & returned to New Mexico. My wife paid Smith's bill: $18,000.

EARLY SEPTEMBER, 1982: I received a phone message asking me to meet an Assistant District Attorney in Lower Manhattan. The meeting was scheduled for late Friday afternoon. It was memorably muggy. The building seemed totally deserted. I walked through airless corridors, past dingy offices & finally came to a room devoid of all furniture, save desk & chair. A young man waited, his feet on the desk.

This was his last day there, he explained. He was entering private practice in Wisconsin. He asked what I knew about the case. Virtually nothing, I said, though I added I'd heard Marin carried a knife & beat his wife.

'Emanuel? He's a pussycat. Keep your fucking mouth shut.' Not another word.

1998: Manuel Marin & his wife were charged with producing & selling fake Calders for $1.5 million. He served time & was released. Meanwhile, the Calder Foundation reports the two are still making fake Calders.

CHAPTER 8　Surrealists

The Surrealists delighted in visual puns. Here a hocker (with disks) shares eyes with a dragon. The image itself never changes. What changes is the observer's organization of its parts.

Tribal artists often shared that delight. This was especially true for native groups in Alaska & Melanesia. Punsters there possessed, in Lévi-Strauss' words, the 'dithyrambic gift of synthesis, the almost monstrous faculty to perceive as similar what all other men have conceived as different.'[1]

The Surrealists did more than create visual puns. They collected examples from distant lands. They saw these as mirrored images of their own vision.

In Europe, museums displayed tribal arts in museums für völkerkunde, behind glass. Suddenly, the Surrealists found themselves in New York, refugees during the Second War, 1940-1945. There they could buy tribal art, often for little.

'All the essentials of humanity's artistic treasures could be found in New York, where samples were constantly bought and sold', wrote Lévi-Strauss. 'If I did not have it before my eyes, it would be hard to believe that I bought one day a sixteenth-century Tuscan sideboard for a few dollars....'[2]

In the early 1940s, on Third Avenue, New York, Max Ernst passed a shop displaying a collection of spoons from many lands. Included was a spoon from the Northwest Coast. The dealer, Julius Carlebach, didn't want to break up the collection. Ernst proposed, instead, that Carlebach assemble a collection of Northwest Coast art. He agreed. He'd heard rumors about a source (Heye).

When the Surrealist Kurt Seligman saw Ernst's new collection, he offered to reveal the source of his witchcraft illustrations in exchange for the shop's address. Ernst declined, judging the exchange uneven. It was only a matter of days, however, before a determined André Breton, spokesman for the Surrealist movement, located that shop.

Where Ernst focused on the Northwest Coast, Breton collected widely, especially from Alaska & Melanesia.[3] So did the Surrealists: Masson, Matta, Tanguy, Duchamp, Calder, Seligmann, Martins, Ford, Donati, as did their friends: Lévi-Strauss, Vanetti, Lebel, Duthuit, Reis.

By 1941, André Breton and his family were on 11th Street, in almost daily contact with Meyer Shapiro who taught at Columbia. Matta was on 9th, Pollock & Onslow Ford on 8th, Kiesler on 14th & Gorky on Union Square.[4] All were unknown, poor. Fame came later. Dolores Vanetti recalled that Duchamp's apartment was so small, the bathroom door had to be closed before opening the front door.[5]

Lévi-Strauss continues: 'Max Ernst, André Breton, Georges Duthuit, and I frequented a small antique shop on Third Avenue which, in response to our demand, became Ali Baba's cave . . . exquisite stone masks from Teotihuancan … magnificent wood carvings from the northwest Pacific coast … [all] regarded merely as ethnographic documents.'[6]

Breton's wife had little interest in hidden treasures. When they changed New York hotels, she checked for bugs, while her impatient husband roamed back streets, curio shops, whatever, arriving back with trophies.[7] He spoke only French, preferring not to degrade pronouncements about Surrealism.

Soon, every Surrealist apartment became a pirate's wardroom: loot from Seven Seas, origins forgotten. They arranged these randomly, letting them collide, ignoring function, culture, history. They hoped accident might reveal analogies convention concealed. One such analogy was the co-existence of contraries.

Breton's later Paris apartment contained so many examples that, just to sit down, much less prepare a meal or sleep or shower, required reorganizing. When space or money ran out, the Surrealists sold their paintings, even traded fur coats for them,[8] but kept their tribal art & took it back to Europe when the War ended.

To Visual Puns, they added Found Art, Hidden Art, Invisible Art, Silent Music,

Motionless Dance, Unworldly Sounds, Ready-made Objects, Natural History Specimens & offered these as 'Witnesses' to the universality of the Surrealist vision.

That vision, they said, wasn't unique to them, but known in remote times, remote lands. Not freaks, not curiosities, declared Breton, but part of the natural order. The Surrealists made the unfamiliar familiar. They destabilized traditions. By their art & by their collections, they expanded our perception of reality.

JULIUS CARLEBACH (1909-1964)

According to Lévi-Strauss, Carlebach's only interests 'were old German chinaware and quaint curios of the gemtülich type. Even when we put him on the right track, he never had more than two or three pieces of tribal art at one time.'[9]

Carlebach entered the family business (Meissen porcelain, Biedermeier furniture) in Germany. The last customer to enter their shop was Hermann Goering, buying furniture for the Air Ministry. In 1937, the family fled, shipping stock to New York as 'household effects.' Initially, Carlebach advised companies assembling furniture for corporate headquarters. Antiques were carried as 'secondhand' (depreciating in five years to 0) – until the IRS objected. Then he & his wife opened a shop on Third Avenue. The chance visit of Max Ernst changed that shop forever. It may even have changed art history. It certainly changed the MAI.

ANNEX VAULTS

The Surrealists first bought from Carlebach. Then, they discovered the Annex. It was, as one of them phrased it, 'a Surrealist Macy's.' Matta told me the story. They raced to the Bronx in two taxis, picking up cases of beer along the way. Turbyfill welcomed them. Now they could choose. They did. They first focused on Yup'ik masks. Imagine a cross between a Calder mobile & a Míro painting. The Yup'ik collection at the MAI was the finest in the world, numbering in the hundreds. Heye called them 'jokes' (his choice of word). He sold these masks to Carlebach for $38 & $54 each. At the Annex, they averaged $15.[10]

André Breton acquired this Kuskokwim mask (opposite) from the Annex, as did Georges Duthuit, art historian for the Surrealist movement. The two represent opposing masks placed on opposite sides of a dance area. (Duthuit mask: upper part should face the other way).

'I was reluctant,' writes Lévi-Strauss, 'to become the owner of such fragile masterpieces and feel responsible for their safekeeping to future generations. I even doubted

that these masks belonged to the solid world of objects. I rather saw them as fleeting and almost immaterial embodiments of words, visions, and beliefs, eluding durable possession.'[11]

Yup'ik carvers rendered songs or stanzas (*apullut*) visually. I'm reminded of Paul Klee who wanted his work to sound like a fairy tale, to be a world where things fall upward. Like the Yup'ik, he preferred the borderless. He said his work owed more to Bach & Mozart than to art.

The eye focuses, observes, from a distance, with detachment. Sound, by contrast, *involves*. It favors sound from any direction. Its essential feature isn't location, but that it be, that it surround. We say, 'The night shall be filled with music', just as the air is filled with fragrance. Locality is irrelevant. The concert enthusiast closes his eyes.

How do you visualize a song? Use an acoustic model. Subvert all other senses. Let the ear command. Let each song, obedient to some inner impulse, create its own dimensions, assert its own identity. No frame, no borders, no up, no down. The ear registers sound simultaneously from all directions.

Flickering oil lamps don't dissolve darkness. They illuminate objects within it. Yup'ik call these 'spirits.' They say they come from memory. They appear. Speak. Then fade back into darkness.

Once used, they're abandoned to the elements or to children. No surviving example dates earlier than the 19th century. Yet both renewal & memory belong to deep time. I regard this tradition as ancient.

Yup'ik masks astonish us in still other ways. Paired examples look alike. This

shouldn't mislead us. Our two hands look alike, but symbolically play opposing roles. So do paired masks. Each assumes an opposing role on either side of a dance 'happening.'

A second type of visual pun occurs. Each represents contraries: male/female, winter/summer, Walrus/Wolf. But winter never fades to summer & Walrus never becomes Wolf. Each retains its identity. Nothing transforms. The Kuskokwim mask, shown here, combines Summer & Winter. These complex masks hung from the ceiling of dance areas. Performers addressed audiences from behind them, as podiums or Seals of Office.

In Lévi-Strauss' essay on Max Ernst, he notes parallels between Ernst's paintings & his own writings. The common feature, he explains, is binary opposition. He quotes Ernst extolling 'the bringing together of two or more elements, apparently opposite in nature, on a level whose nature is the opposite of theirs.' He illustrates this with Ernst's 'chance encounter' of a sewing machine [binder] & umbrella [blocker] on a dissecting table normally reserved for organic objects.[12]

NORTHWEST COAST ART

After selecting Yup'ik masks, the Surrealists moved happily through the Northwest Coast vaults, choosing masterpiece after masterpiece.

Unlike Yup'ik traditions, Northwest Coast artists began with borders, then locked every motif in place. Each belonged to a tightly-structured, highly-competitive community. Surely it's no accident their most successful creations were containers.[13]

Only in masked ceremonies do identities change. Observers watch with wonder as masks with strings & hinges changed before their eyes. Ceremonies re-create an age of extraordinary events & noble deeds. In the words of Bill Reid, Haida carver, men lived as equals with mythic beasts & the play of Raven & Eagle, Frog & Beaver, Thunderbird & Whale, established all that was to be.

In depicting this, Northwest Coast carvers sometimes show two beings occupying a single space by sharing parts. Such visual puns do more than show complexity: they depict transformation. Before one's eyes, Bear becomes Wolf, then Bear again. This was wholly consistent with Northwest Coast thought. A Kwakiutl legend tells of the mythic hero who first appears as a whale & later as a man disembarking from the whale, which is no longer himself but his canoe. When he meets the local chief & his daughter, whom he wishes to marry, he presents them with the whale, which has returned to its animal nature at the end of its third transmutation.

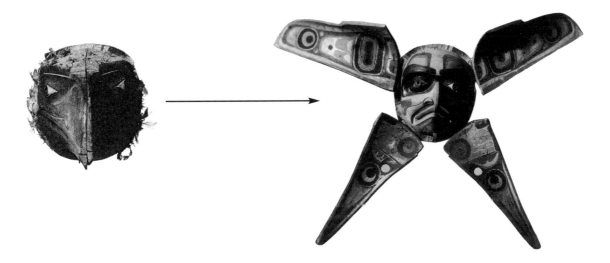

This single feature, above all others, proved to be the most difficult for early ethnologists to understand. When told a carving represented a bear & later told it represented a whale, they assumed an error. It remained for the Surrealists to explain.

BETTY PARSONS GALLERY

Several Surrealists, including Max Ernst, with Barnett Newman writing the catalog, exhibited 'Northwest Coast Indian Painting', at the Betty Parsons Gallery, New York, 1946. There they displayed ex-Heye pieces, now in their own collections, plus 18 borrowed from the AMNH. That museum had, on public display, a wealth of Northwest Coast objects, every piece identified by function. By taking them off display at the AMNH & exhibiting them a mile away, the Surrealists didn't deny their ethnography, but celebrated them as art.

True, the Surrealists just stripped the MAI of one masterpiece after another. But they liberated American Indian art from centuries of neglect. They put it out there for the world to see.

In 1941, the Museum of Modern Art exhibited Indian Art in the United States, complete with a Utah pictograph reproduced full-size, 60 feet x 12 feet. The installation, by René d'Harnoncourt, was said to be masterful: 'One came upon the mural on leaving the confines of "dark ceremonial chambers."'[14]

A letter from these times, written by Carl Schuster (1904-1969), during the Second War, was addressed to a friend in London. On the last day of each month, Schuster sent soap, socks, tea, jam, etc. His letter explained the one-day delay: Miguel Covarrubias had arrived unexpectedly, bringing with him 'the young Rockefeller' [Nelson] & 'a tall Czech or Hungarian count [René d'Harnoncourt].'

That Covarrubias, Rockefeller & d'Harnoncourt sought out Carl Schuster, late that rainy night, in a tiny room in an unfashionable part of New York, testifies to the erudition of this quiet scholar.

Carl uncorked a bottle of wine he'd saved for victory. They talked until 3 a.m. What they talked about was creating a museum of tribal arts. I cannot think of four more qualified to address that question. From their discussion came New York's Museum of Primitive Art & its successor, the Rockefeller wing of the Metropolitan Museum of Art.[15]

CARLEBACH GALLERIES

Julius Carlebach moved to Madison Avenue, northwest corner of East 79th Street: on the ground floor, with 7 windows, all filled with tribal arts & chess sets. Young people paused. There were larger galleries, of course, selling more expensive works. Still, in 1964, Carlebach's prices reached $50,000, an unheard of sum then for tribal art. Carlebach opened a branch: Altman Gallery, Los Angeles.

George Heye sold to Carlebach & bought from him. He even advised him on pre-Columbian purchases & did so, not for glory or ego, but cash. Carlebach, in turn, complained 'that Heye was bossy, and ruthless in negotiating a deal.'[16]

'This', said Bird, 'was real praise. The rapport grew to the point where Julius sold George items in three figures just on the basis of a description over the phone. I think it helps account for the Carlebach Galleries stunning morale.'[17]

In 1953, Heye wrote to Carlebach: 'As you know, you and I have had many most agreeable relations in a business way and also personal, so I venture to bring to your notice one little point. The only weakness I have ever found in our many dealings together is the fact that you are very weak on many of your specimens that I am familiar with as regards location.

'Right now I have quite a few pieces [six] that we would love to have but they are not of any value to us unless we can find out where they were found; so, I am beginning to get quite impatient about either returning them to you or keeping them in the hope that you can find out [countries of origin].'[18]

Heye wasn't seeking the context from which specimens came. No, no. As the MAI cataloger, he simply wanted to know 'country of origin', nothing more. After fifty years as the world's leading collector of American Indian artifacts, after close association with some of the world's leading anthropologists, he still didn't get the point.

Heye died, 1957, aged 84. Carlebach died, 1964, aged 55. His New York gallery closed. But, in a strange way, it lived on. The delivery boy there became a dealer.

Iroquois Figurine

Suppose someone found, in a proto-historic Iroquois grave, a 16th century French spoon, its handle shaped like a modest maiden. 'Obviously the model', we would say.

No such find has ever been reported. We can only guess what inspired 16th & 17th century Iroquois to carve figurines of modest nudes, wear them as pendants & bury them with their dead, principally women & children.[1]

Many years ago, I worked in a remote part of the Western District, Papua New Guinea. Trade objects were rare: isolated villages treasured a steel knife or mirror scrap. Few men & no women had ever seen a European, yet for at least 60 years all had heard stories about distant strangers. A few men, visiting distant villages, actually saw those strangers. Yet decades before the first government patrol entered those villages, their inhabitants began to change, partly because of trade & partly because of ideas. Both trade & fashions reached them via intertribal routes. I thought of 16th century Iroquois villages.

As early as 1529, European maps included accurate details of the Atlantic Coast. These maps were drawn, their authors acknowledge, with the help of native pilots & cartographers. Once ashore, European trade objects moved rapidly inland, carried over vast distances via ancient networks of trade & alliance. Indians served as middle men.

European goods reached the Iroquois well ahead of explorers. So did ideas. Long before missionaries arrived, graves were reoriented. Burial offerings multiplied. Mortuary changes began with the first appearance of trade goods. Behind these changes lay, I suspect, fear of death.

Traditionally, the Iroquois believed in reincarnation. Life, they asserted, was an unending trail of rebirths. Their first encounter with the concept of death — as full stop — must have been traumatic. Those who take reincarnation for granted seem especially vulnerable. Resurrection offers the *possibility* of a single, spiritual reawakening in another world — hardly reassuring to anyone expecting endless rebirths in this world. The shift, from reincarnation to resurrection, produced profound changes for many people, including the Iroquois.

POST-CONTACT

All Iroquoian figurines are post-Contact. No prehistoric example is known. Many look so Hellenistic, so non-Indian, that a European model seems required. Except for a rare headdress or possible mask, they seem completely alien to Iroquois iconography, even to North American Indian art generally. Nothing even remotely like them occurred in the Northeast until after European contact.

Two figurines come from the Adams site in western New York. This is the earliest known Seneca village with trade goods (ca. 1570-1590). Jesuit missionaries arrived 60-80 years after the Adams figures were carved. By then, this tradition was already fading.

The first *recorded* European, Etienne Brulé, 1615-1618, reached the Seneca decades after the Adams site closed. Yet foreigners were already present in Seneca villages. Four Caucasian skeletons occurred at the Dutch Hollow site (ca. 1609-1620), plus a female skeleton with Negroid traits at the Tram site (circa 1570-1590).[2]

POPULARITY

How popular were figurines? Very. All northern Iroquois groups made them, especially the Cayuga & Seneca. The Heye example comes from the Wenro, an Erie group west of the Seneca (the Goodyear site?). It lay in an ash bed along Buffalo Creek, East Elma. The figure is 10 cm, nude, with the hair in a braid.

Not all of these figures enjoy Hellenistic posture, but enough do so that local archeologists call them collectively 'September Morn' figures. This refers to Paul Chabas' coy bather, whose Venus-like portrait — one hand over breasts, the other over genitals — appeared in the 1930s as White Rock beverage ads.

None have clothing. Gender reveals itself by a vulva or phallus, breasts, pregnancy, tress or braid. These are by no means always present. Several figurines, in classic Venus posture, exhibit headgear unsuitable for Iroquois women. One figurine covers its face with its hands. Others have hands at their sides. This lack of uniformity suggests an alien motif, newly introduced. I miss the conformity I associate with traditional iconography.

Within decades, proto-historic Iroquois saw a wide variety of European images on coins, medallions, banners, escutcheons, perhaps porcelains, even embroideries. They recycled some. Not all came through friendly trade. One Seneca grave contained a guidon. Back from battle, Europeans & Indians alike exhibited trophies & copied one another's clothing.

NUDITY

The Vatican Library contains 16th century engravings of Adam & Eve, modestly posed. Some were intended for overseas proselytizing. Nudity became a theological issue when Columbus discovered America. Had he discovered humans not of Adam's seed? Such a discovery challenged biblical authority. It also denied American Indians redemption.

The Vatican supported monogenesis. Years earlier, St. Augustine had scornfully dismissed antipodal man as 'exceedingly absurd.' Indians, the Vatican now declared, were naked innocents, created in God's image. That is exactly how they were first represented, 1493, in a printed announcement of Columbus' discovery.

SCULPTURAL

Recently, a cast-iron handle for a spoon or (less likely) a dagger, was recovered from the Fox site, a Seneca village (ca. 1658-1672). It depicts a hunter grasping the muzzle of a grounded musket, with a dog at the opposite side. More than any other specimen, this tightly rendered sculpture makes me suspect that the model for September Morn figures was sculpture, not print. Iroquoian figurines are three-dimensional, a form not easily derived from flat art.

We don't know what Jacques Cartier left behind in Canada (1534-1543). But we do know that spoons with modest maidens were then popular in France.

Few artists, even great artists, view the world with pristine eyes. Most recycle. In the Marquesas, Paul Gauguin visited the Taipi Valley, set up his easel before a massive, ancient sculpture, then copied a sketch of that sculpture printed in a travel book he took along. He improved on the sketch, but retained several of its errors.

We may never know what inspired the Iroquois to carve images of a modest maiden. One study concluded that Seneca examples symbolized witchcraft, not modesty, and power, not chastity.

I prefer to imagine that Eve appeared among the Iroquois, bringing solace & comfort to mothers in days of sorrow & anxiety.

GREED

by Edmund Carpenter

CHAPTER 1 Deaccessioning

IRS

In 1951, the Internal Revenue Service formally determined that the MAI was exempt from federal taxes. It thereby imbued the public with an interest in its collection. Neither Heye nor any successor could ever again even pretend to deal with its assets as private property. Any attempt to ignore the public interest was litigation waiting to happen.

This didn't happen for a long time. First, Heye traded. If done for scholarly purposes, this was legal, desirable. But, after 1928, he used the Trust to fund Operations. Proceeds from sales rarely went to Acquisitions. Most went to Maintenance & Operations. Every sale depleted the trust, specimen by specimen.

On rare, rare occasions, Heye informed his Board what he was up to. In 1932, they authorized the sale of 143 'duplicate specimens' to the William Rockhill Nelson Trust of Kansas City for $13,600, though these specimens had actually been shipped the previous year. Board approval mattered little.

An unstated portion of these funds (listed as 'contributions') was added to the Collections Account. The Expeditions Account got $3500. The rest went to Operations. A second sale to the Nelson Trust brought the total number of specimens to 300. Records of this additional sale exist in Kansas City, but not in New York.[1]

In May of that year, Frederick Hodge wrote to Heye: 'I should think you would be able to conduct a good deal more field work this year from the proceeds of the Museum collection, which I am told, amounted to many thousands of dollars.'[2] Four days later, Heye replied: 'I only wish it were true.... If you know of anyone who wants to buy "thousands of dollars worth", believe me, we have plenty of duplicates to sell and would be glad to do it.'[3]

Heye didn't know that the librarian at the Huntington Free Library kept Hodge informed of Heye's activities.

At first, Heye sold modestly. For years, he'd bought from Charles Ratton in Paris. Now he sold to him. In 1934, he sent Ratton pre-Columbian material, then 100 ethnographic pieces. Heye valued artifacts by their cost to him. When he sold, he roughly doubled the price paid. A mask costing Heye $15, cost Ratton $38.

In 1942, Heye recommended to his Board 'the sale of duplicate and surplus specimens of the Collection . . . of no additional scientific value to your Institution in connection with the study of Anthropology.' He assured his Board that he'd never before sold 'surplus material, though fully authorized to do so under the terms of said Foundation Deed.' In fact, he'd sold since 1928, though not on the level that followed.

Heye had recently met Julius Carlebach. The MAI never recovered. Consider just one category. In 1940, MAI had the world's finest collection of Yup'ik Eskimo masks from Alaska. Of these, Kuskokwim examples, assembled by Amos Twitchell, were exceptional. In 1919, Heye bought 55 masks from Twitchell. Heye dismissed them as 'jokes' (his word). From 1944 to 1946, Carlebach purchased 26, at $38 & $54 each. The MAI now has 18 out of the original 55.[4] During the 1940s, Carlebach purchased at least 64 Yup'ik masks, including 2 masks Gordon collected on the Kuskokwim, 5 from Goodnews Bay & 16 from Anik.[5]

By 1942, Heye became *the* leading dealer in Indian artifacts. Perhaps he'd always been a dealer. He certainly enjoyed secrecy, the mark of many dealers. He also enjoyed bettering others. He loved to dicker, out-maneuver, make a profit, however small. It gave him something to do, some place to go.

HEYE'S WILL

When he died, 1957, he endowed the museum with $1.5m. By 1976, endowment totaled $4,012,359. Judiciously used, it might have protected what was left. Heye's immediate successor, E. K. Burnett, watched expenses, kept honest records & left the collection alone. In 1960, just before he retired, he warned the Trustees, *sub rosa*, that Frederick Dockstader not succeed him.

FREDERICK DOCKSTADER (? – 1998)

But Dockstader did. He became Director & served in that capacity from 1960 to 1975. Heye hired him in 1955, after Dockstader voluntarily identified *kachina* dolls in the MAI collection. Heye was delighted: 'This is the first time in years that anybody has taken the pains to help make my collection more valuable for others.'[6] Heye died two years later, after crippling strokes.

Heye's eccentricities were nothing compared to Dockstader's. Gifted as a crafts-man, he filled holes in Mimbres pots (though these 'spirit' holes were intended as such); repainted Kuskokwim masks (best left untouched); enameled two house posts& lintel; etc. He couldn't leave specimens alone.

The moment he became Director, his ambitions were unrestrained. He gave three philanthropists masterpieces. None reciprocated. He tried media celebrities: Dick Cavett, Marlon Brando, Andy Warhol, John Huston, even Huston's son, Tony. Noth-ing came of that.

So he sold, traded or gave away thousands of pieces each year. Most survive, else-where of course. Most still bear Heye catalog numbers. But only a few can be reunited with their histories. Field records were discarded; catalog entries falsified; associated objects scattered. I list below some of the routes by which those specimens left the MAI:

EXITS

1/ At Audubon Terrace, in the Museum Shop, postcards & souvenirs were in front, with blankets & *kachinas* behind. A basement room was reserved for dealers, collec-tors, celebrities. The exhibition area had study collections, below display cases, in locked drawers. After the Museum closed, dealers bid.

2/ Most of the collection lay in the Annex. Dealers from London, Victoria, Denver, Los Angeles, were welcome. Scholars: by appointment.

3/ The May Company mounted a HUGE sale of Northwest Coast art. Stock came from the Annex, arranged by a dealer, then a May Company employee. The first ex-hibit opened in Kansas City. From there it traveled to other May stores (Los Angeles, Denver, etc). A full-page ad appeared in the *Los Angeles Times*. Sales were so success-ful, stock was constantly replaced.

4/ During the 1970s, the MAI had a ground-floor booth in Bloomingdale's Depart-ment Store, New York. An ad in *The New York Times*, featured this event. I recall a Plains shirt offered for $25,000, an unheard of price at the time. It went unsold. It & others were returned to the Annex. This created a problem. The MAI had duplicate catalogs at Audubon Terrace & the Annex. Cards at the Annex were stamped *EX-CHANGED*, but not those at Audubon Terrace. Unsold pieces were returned to the Annex or transferred to the Museum Shop storage.[7]

5/ William Stiles, Chief Curator, ran a mail order business with mimeographed catalogs. Stock came from the Annex. Stiles' field-collecting was financed by a tax-free grant to the MAI from Stanley Grant, then Chairman of the Board. Grant was allowed to choose anything he wanted from what Stiles assembled.

6/ One gallery on the Upper East side of Manhattan specialized in MAI specimens. These came directly from the Annex. So did American Indian & Eskimo pieces sold by Everett Rassiga. ▓▓▓▓▓ ▓▓▓▓▓▓▓▓, Carlebach's delivery boy, now associated with Rassiga, sold ex-Heye pieces from residences in Denver, New York, London. To these, he added stock from the Denver Art Museum, Brooklyn Museum, as well as from other American & English museums.

7/ Stanley Grant & Frederick Dockstader accompanied MAI touring exhibits. Collectors, invited to opening nights, obtained delivery after shows closed.

8/ A retired Admiral, Providence, Rhode Island, inherited a small but fine collection of early Navaho blankets. The MAI urged their donation. When they arrived, they went directly to the Museum Shop & sold within hours. One Trustee called his purchase 'a great bargain.'

SELLING

Selling didn't end with Dockstader's dismissal. A court order prohibiting the removal of any object from the MAI was lifted. Curt Muser, Chairman of the Board, permitted Heye objects to be sold by the Museum Shop. Monies went to operations. Selling wasn't discontinued until 6.29.77, when the Collections Committee banned this practice.[8] Even then, as we shall see, it didn't end.

Christian Cross

In 17th century Iroquois graves, brandy jugs often commingle with Jesuit rings & Christian crosses. Many Indians regarded alcohol as a spiritual blessing.

Francois Vachon de Belmont (1645-1732), a missionary near Montreal, wrote that intoxicated Indians experienced 'a new sort of elation that promptly and effectively achieved the end of taking them out of themselves.'[1] Dream-cultivation & dream-submission dominated traditional life. Dreams could be induced by seclusion, fasting, meditation. Dreamers asked others to interpret their dreams.

Temporary loss of reason wasn't regarded as sacrilege. By getting outside of the social order, they believed they could get inside a higher spiritual order. Extreme situations had more validity than normal ones. True reality lay beyond established patterns. A drunken trance became a revelation. They cultivated excess through ecstasy, frenzy, drunkenness. As excess lost intensity, it became less valuable.

17th century Iroquois rode their emotions bareback under the protection of alcohol. Then, in 1800, their prophet Handsome Lake combined Quaker teachings with elements of the old faith. In one version of his Good Message, 5 out of 130 sections appealed for abstinence.[2] However, in the first centuries after First Contact, few promoted temperance & many supported excess.

The Iroquois sought to break through into another order of experience. They sought to escape all sensory boundaries. They valued frenzy. For spiritual power, they turned to drunkenness. It made them, for a moment, one with truth. They honored alcohol as they had long honored tobacco.

TOBACCO & ALCOHOL

This Christian cross, engraved by Pierre Huquet, Montreal silversmith, was intended for Indian trade. That same combination, pipe & liquor, occurs on many North American Indian pipes, including those in the MAI collection. In one such pipe, the carver shows a bear deity offering a keg of liquor to an Indian.

'When', continues Belmont, 'they have only enough brandy to induce drunkenness for only one, if four are present, three will not even take a taste. But one will be chosen to have the privilege of becoming inebriated. Many say that they cannot be intoxicated on a single glass of brandy, that there is only one degree of drunkenness worthwhile, the sort they call "Gannontioaratonseri", complete insobriety. When they begin to feel the effects of brandy, they rejoice, shout-

ing, "Good, good, my head is reeling." Then they begin to chant their "Gannonhaoury", into which they put all of the evil which comes to mind.'[3]

They were not 'ashamed of so infamous a vice',[4] but took pride in getting drunk and in making others drunk',[5] for 'to be drunk is to be valiant.'[6] The Jesuits never sought to impose abstinence,[7] though 'Drunkenness, dreams and Impurity',[8] constituted major obstacles to conversion.

Abbé Belmont begins with the observation that insobriety in Europe, which is 'looked upon as a mark of good-fellowship, a source of pleasure and comfort which friends and convivial companions allow themselves', should not be confused with Indian drunkenness, which is '. . . a peculiar kind of insobriety.'[9]

'Insobriety among Savages was quite a different species than the same weakness among Europeans. For the Savages, having found a beverage which could so quickly and efficaciously enliven their dullness, take them out of themselves and give them thereby the ability and the bravado they desired, it was not long before drunkards could be seen killing one another, husbands burning their wives, women disgracing their husbands, fathers throwing their children into burning caldrons.

'They saved brandy until they have collected enough to make themselves drunk. Then they take to drinking without eating (for eating would inhibit the effects of the brandy). When they feel their heads beginning to swim, they rejoice and start to chant their death song into which they pour all their imprecations against their enemies. Once inebriated, they throw off their clothing, or let it drop, and running about the town naked, beat one another. They bite each other's noses and ears, so there are few whole, entire visages remaining. They run about howling with knives in their hands; they delight in seeing their women and children fleeing before them, as if they were masters of the World.'[10]

Then Abbé Belmont lists, with details, atrocities committed by drunken natives.[11] Two centuries later, details still make frightening reading. This was no exception. In 1642, Father Richard wrote that the Iroquois 'did not buy our liquors on account of any pleasant taste . . . but simply to become intoxicated.'[12] Father Carheil, 1668, said the Cayuga 'drink only to intoxicate themselves; they say so openly, and sing their intentions to do so, before executing it, and that they are heard to shout, "I am going to lose my head; I am going to drink of the water that takes one's wits away."'[13]

DREAM OBEDIENCE

Alcohol was used to cultivate dreams. To the ancient rite of dream recitation was added the drink-all party. 'Generally all savages drink to intoxicate themselves', wrote one observer. 'It has become the basis of the religion.'[14]

'All that they dream,' wrote Father Bruyas in 1668, 'must be carried out.'[15] Since dream commands weren't personal wishes, but divine orders, no one was held responsible for acts committed in obedience to them. Abbé Belmont, in a hypothetical dialog between priest &

pagan, has the Indian say, 'Drunkenness excuses everything.'[16] Missionaries & traders alike described scores of cases where those who committed serious crimes enjoyed impunity because they were intoxicated.

Accounts of dream-guessing & dream-obedience, rich in detail & variation, occur repeatedly in the *Jesuit Relations*. It's tempting to quote them. But my point is simple: to the Iroquois, intoxication originally meant, not flight, but search; not escape, but fulfillment; not loss of self, but discovery of self. To them, it was a positive experience, a powerful communion. In 1757, Iroquois women from three tribes requested rum from Sir William Johnson 'for Christenings, Weddings, Dreams, Burials &c' and 'to fulfill some Dreams.'[17]

CHAPTER 2 Investigation

I served as a trustee of the MAI from 1973-1985. I may have been elected for the wrong reason. It was an uncomfortable association. I can't tell that story in every detail, for I know only what I experienced. But let me describe the highlights as I remember them.

At my first Board meeting, the Shop Manager announced — to warm applause — a quarterly profit of over $200,000. I wondered: from postcards?

At a later Board meeting, the Director stated he'd had an offer of $55,000 for a set of Kwakiutl house posts. I knew they were already on the market for $130,000. I spoke to the Chairman of the Board, Stanley Grant. He dismissed my concern: 'Just give me two numbers [catalog numbers] of anything you feel was improperly deaccessioned.'

I did. One was a Salish spindle whorl; the other a Kuskokwim mask. Grant said the spindle whorl had been stolen by a former MAI curator, now at another museum. In fact, it was still in the MAI, for sale. Grant himself acquired the second piece. He said

he'd purchased it years before from the dealer Klejman, for $1000. In fact, he'd purchased it recently from the Museum Shop, on a Sunday, for $70. After his death, it sold for $90,000.[1]

On advice of counsel, I went to the New York State Attorney General (NY-AG). An account of my complaint appeared in *The New York Times*, March 3, 1974. The next meeting of the Board, four days later, proved awkward.

CENTURY CLUB

We dined around a circular table. One trustee left his chair, moved behind me & knocked me to the floor. As I stood up, I glanced around the table. Most trustees looked stunned, but four smirked. John Ewers, Smithsonian ethnologist, concentrated on his soup.

John Williams separated us. This disappointed one of the Trustees: 'That would have been an interesting fight', then she added, as an aside to me, 'I don't think you would have come out too well.'

In the official minutes of that meeting, this reads: 'In particular, Mr. ██████████ took extremely strong vocal and other exception to the actions and remarks of Dr. Carpenter. For a brief period parliamentary procedures were suspended, during which various extracurricular endeavors by the two Trustees were first moderated and then terminated with the assistance of Mr. Williams....'

Later in that long evening I moved that deaccessioning be suspended. 'The motion was seconded by two trustees, each of whom stated the seconding did not indicate support of the substance of the motion.' Motion tabled.

The meeting ended at 3 am. When I left, 43rd Street was empty, save for ████ ████████, hurrying away. I caught up: '████, could we find some place for coffee?'

'Carpenter', he replied, 'life is positional power and you haven't got it.'

LOUIS J. LEFKOWITZ

The New York State Attorney General sought the removal of several trustees. He also asked the court to compel the trustees to account for the Museum's assets, to surcharge them for damages & to rescind all transactions constituting self-dealing between the Museum & any present or former trustees. Finally, he charged the Board with having violated its fiduciary responsibilities by delegating them to Dockstader.

At which point, five trustees resigned, including Stanley Grant, Chairman of the Board. John Williams became Chairman. Four generations of the Williams family had served on the MAI Board.

Williams immediately discovered, by chance, that Dockstader had repeatedly violated a court order prohibiting the removal of artifacts from the MAI. Williams changed locks, notified the Court & asked Counsel to telegraph the Board: SPECIAL MEETING ALL TRUSTEES AT JOHN P CAMPBELL OFFICES, 100 WALL ST, 9:15 AM, WEDNESDAY MAY 15. SUBJECT: DEACCESSIONING DR FREDERICK J DOCKSTADER.

Williams reported to the Board: 'A can of worms. Debts, including *publishing* debts. Don't ask for details.' Dockstader, however, wasn't dismissed for violating a court order. Trustees might have been liable. Instead, counsel placed before the Board applications he'd made for passport, driver's license, retirement, etc. Each bore different ages & places of birth. Asked to explain, Dockstader, represented by counsel, remained silent. The Chair said, 'You went too far.' The Director was dismissed.

A short time later, John Williams took his life. He was a big man, young, handsome, about to be married. Lefkowitz stepped in & reconstituted the MAI Board.

I was the only trustee reappointed. I then worked at the Museum für Völkerkunde, Basel. Though I attended all Board meetings, I didn't participate in planning. This was undertaken by Curt Muser. At the first meeting of the new Board, I nominated him as Chairman. He, in turn, nominated James O'Rorke as Vice Chairman. I knew neither. At that same meeting, the new Vice Chairman moved that Lord Day Lord replace Curtis Mallet. The motion passed.

Hardly an auspicious beginning: bankrupt museum, missing much of its collection, now facing an investigation that took years.

SACKLER INVESTIGATION

Dockstader met Dr. Arthur Sackler — entrepreneur, collector, philanthropist — in the early 1960s. Sackler gave the MAI $15-20,000, 1962-65. Dockstader testified 'when money was needed . . . he [offered to] pay.' His wife was then on the MAI Board. On the basis of Sackler's promise, Dockstader committed $125,000. Sackler's checks were slow: 'business troubles.' By 1977, a deficit of $28,000 was carried on the MAI books as 'account receivable.'

Museum records listed over 100 items deaccessioned to Sackler. Their cost was added to the 'Sackler Account.' That account, Dockstader testified, was treated as 'tax deductible', though purchased by Dr. Sackler. No payment for them had yet been received.

Though most of the pieces in the basement storeroom 'appear to belong to Dr. Sackler', the Attorney General noted, scores bore MAI numbers, yet didn't correspond to catalog entries. They did correspond, however, to a 1965 document entitled *Archeological Specimens Released to Dr. Arthur Sackler*. 'There is no evidence of payment . . . some [are] mislabeled. The purpose of this mislabeling is not clear.' Their value was judged 'substantial.'

Twelve years earlier, on Dockstader's advice, Sackler purchased, for $25,000, the remaining stock of 'The Pinata Party', a Greenwich Village shop specializing in Peruvian folk art & textiles. Everything was now stored in the basement room, Audubon Terrace. Sackler installed metal racks. Only Dockstader & Sackler's curator had keys.

In 1974, a locksmith opened that door. Inside, investigators found Peruvian souvenirs & pre-Columbian masterworks. Some numbers on the Heye pieces had been removed, but were faintly visible. These same Heye numbers appeared on Peruvian souvenirs offered for sale in the Museum Shop. About a dozen specimens undergoing this transformation were saved for possible prosecution. The rest was returned to Sackler.

Several years later, Joel Cooper, Attorney General's office, phoned me in Basel where I worked. He asked that this evidence be released. I said I wouldn't *oppose* any decision the AG made in this matter, but wanted no part of it. He didn't press.

A week later, John Doar, who represented me, called to say a court document required my signature. It bore the signature of Roland Force, newly appointed MAI Director. The court, however, needed my signature. I had no idea what it concerned. I returned immediately to New York. The document turned out to be the release form Cooper had requested. That someone — court clerk, judge — spotted the substitution — a miracle, at least in New York.

A meeting was called at Lord Day Lord. They represented both Sackler & the MAI.[2] I've never, before or since, seen so many lawyers assembled. Robert Abrams, the Attorney General, presided. He had decided not to prosecute Dockstader. Evidence against Sackler remained unclear.

Still, Sackler failed to explain the basement workshop. Heye objects, recently sold at auction under another name, were traced to him. His private collection, without explanation, contained ex-Heye pieces. Many were pre-Columbian masterpieces. Sackler wanted this evidence released to him. The AG was sick of the case. Just sign.

All eyes turned toward me. I have no gift for such moments. But, miraculously, the right words came: 'You wouldn't let a Black boy get away with this.' The meeting disbanded, silently.

■■■■■ INVESTIGATION

Marshall Saville's excavations in Ecuador produced much gold & silver. In the course of that work, he mapped tombs & opened about half of them. Samuel Lothrop saw these maps when he worked for Heye. After Heye's death, he asked about them.

Dockstader replied that he couldn't find them. Yet he did, immediately. A decade later, he turned them over to ■■■■■ ■■■■■.[3] Dockstader provided a letter identifying ■■■■■ as an MAI archeologist. The letter guaranteed that the MAI, as a public museum, would preserve all finds, all records.

In Quito, ■■■■■ contacted the owner of the hacienda where Saville dug. He proved to be a Swiss national, with twin nephews in Basel. ■■■■■ signed an agreement with him. Using Saville's maps, he opened the first tomb. Its contents brought the equivalent of $125,000 USD in a Zürich gallery.

▓▓▓▓▓, mistaking my wife & me for potential buyers, telephoned from Vancouver. I then worked at the Museum für Völkerkunde, Basel. My wife & I lunched with ▓▓▓▓▓, together with one of the twin nephews of the hacienda owner. The nephew worked at the office of the Basel prosecutor.

▓▓▓▓▓ began the lunch by showing us Dockstader's letter (the AG also found a copy in the MAI files). He told us how he'd cashed his assets, moved to Ecuador, married a local girl, then struck a deal with the hacienda owner. He explained how these objects reached Switzerland: via U.S. diplomatic pouch.

After lunch, we were invited to view, in a nearby village, the second tomb's contents. Gold objects covered a table top 3' x 2'. These were shortly sold at a Zürich gallery.

In 1972-73, a Basel charity associated with the prosecutor's office, paid the equivalent of $50,000 USD for 34 pre-Columbian ceramic figures from Ecuador. These were then donated to the Museum für Völkerkunde. A curator there judged most to be fakes.

INVENTORY

A court-ordered inventory was undertaken. Losses proved immense. In *The Heye & the Mighty*, Roland Force argues that Heye, as donor, had the right to sell. He did not. State law governed that trust. Changes in the trust required Board & Attorney General approval. In some cases, it required court approval.

Heye ignored all this, though he kept some records. Dockstader kept none, unless we count falsified records. He provided no records at all for 15,997 missing specimens. He created fictitious documents; manufactured false rubber stamps[4] (an Assistant Attorney General found the machine that made them); submitted misleading reports. For ten years, auditors refused to sign the books. The National Science Foundation placed the MAI on five years' probation for misuse of grant funds.

The inventory was financed by the Rock Foundation, where I served as Vice-President.[5] Teams re-catalogued thousands of unique objects. The MAI was then looking for another home. No one wanted a collection missing thousands of key pieces. For decades the inventory was suppressed, even from the funding source. I first saw a copy 25 years later when preparing this book.

Dockstader estimated 4.5 million specimens. He warned of spears tipped with poison & masks dipped in arsenic. If he intended to sabotage the inventory, he failed. Not the 4.5m he claimed, not even the 1.5m Force claimed during negotiations with the AMNH. Instead: 676,605 were *inventoried*; 26,992 listed as 'deaccessioned'; 15,997 as 'missing.' Officially, about 43,000 pieces 'departed.' Yet we know, from the Surrealists' records alone, that Heye failed to record many sales. Dockstader recorded nothing.[6]

There are roughly three pieces per catalog card, with about 246,000 cards. A pair of moccasins counts as two; a full costume as many; quiver with arrows as. . .? All estimates are guesses. My guess: between 62,000 - 91,000 specimens left the MAI after 1928. For 50 years they constituted the primary source of American Indian artifacts.

Dealers played an increasing role at the MAI after 1928. Ultimately, they strip-mined that collection. Many occupied strategic positions in the art world. Dealers & senior staff at the MAI partied together. The attorney general's investigation reported that a guard, on duty nights at Audubon Terrace, told friends: 'Come. There's a party tonight at the Indian Museum. Watch through the sky-light. . . .'[7]

INVENTORY PROBLEMS

One of the trustees assigned a former business associate, Alexander Draper, to take over the inventory. It took four years. Force, as the new Director, soon replaced Draper. Computer problems plagued the inventory. Dr. Anna Roosevelt, MAI Curator, delivered a paper at the annual meeting of the American Anthropological Association, 1985: 'poor accounting control . . . original work sheets . . . never entered . . . computer tapes . . . lost or erased.'

In the meantime, some 200 inventoried artifacts entered the art market, secretly. All, without exception, were masterpieces selected by a single dealer. The head of the inventory staff, dying of AIDS, admitted guilt. He was dismissed & died. He was never prosecuted. He made no restitution. The Board was never informed. The FBI limited their search to 3 pieces. More likely, it was over 200 pieces.

At this time, the law firm Lord Day Lord prepared a 27-page brief. They argued that the Trust Deed permitted sales to cover expenses. They accepted Heye's definition of 'scientific value' & 'advancement of Anthropology', ignoring the fact that New York State law governed that trust. Whoever authorized this Lord Day Lord brief concealed it from the Board. Again, I first saw a copy 25 years later, when preparing this book.

WALKING AWAY

Of those who allegedly profited from illegal dealings at the MAI, none were charged. Four were trustees.[8] One is now honored as a philanthropist. Dealers made 'killings.' One dealer alone made & kept millions.

Naxnóx

Shaman's mask representing Naxnóx, a woman's spirit, made by a Tsimshian (Niska) carver, 1790-1840. Its catalog entry reads:

> 'Mask representing a woman's spirit
> that lives at the base of cliff where
> the Nass river current meets the tide.
>
> Nishga
> Kin-colith,
> Nass River B.C.
> Collected by
> Lieut. G. T. Emmons'

Naxnóx reflects 'unwieldy or supernatural power associated with chiefly might, antisocial acts, and distinctive tendencies intended to instill fear in onlookers.'[1] A Naxnóx ceremony involves much masking, much costuming.

Graphite covers the mask. A sharp, bifurcating ridge descends from forehead to mouth. An articulated labret enlarges the lower lip. That lip, now perforated, is an early replacement. The original attachment was probably tanned hide (a scrap remains). The lower lip simulated speaking.

Emmons sold this mask to Heye, 1905-1906, probably for around $15. In 1934, Heye sold it to Charles Ratton, Paris, as one of 100 American Indian artifacts. If Heye was consistent, he roughly doubled their prices.

Ratton exhibited many of these in *Surrealism and Tribal Art*, a show mounted in his Paris gallery, 1936. Few sold. Surrealism wasn't in fashion, least of all in Europe. Nor was tribal art. The Nazis condemned both.

In 1938, Ratton sold this mask, as part of a group, to Adolf Hoffmeister, a cartoonist & Surrealist, then resident in Prague. Included in that group were two ex-Heye pieces, along with 12 Oceanic pieces.

The Surrealists celebrated tribal art & taught the West to recognize masterpieces. In 1999, this mask, at auction, brought over $750,000.[2] In 1944, Heye sold a Kuskokwim mask for $54. Forty years later, it brought $475,000.

Dealers knew the MAI collection offered, in Heye's phrase, 'a killing.'

CHAPTER 3   Texas

Museums of natural history existed in the 17th & 18th centuries, though few in number & little more than curio cabinets. That changed with Darwin's observation, that all life belongs to a common order, subject to common principles. It created natural history museums. From this came museums that openly challenged unnatural history (freaks, oddities) & super-natural history (miracles, relic shrines). The first Gibraltar skull, 1848, was a curiosity until *The Origin of Species*, 1859, allowed it to be seen as part of the natural order.

We honor Darwin, not for the theory of evolution, which pre-dated him by centuries; nor for natural selection, credit rightly going to Alfred Russell Wallace, but for his notion of a single order. All natural science rests on that principle. The alternative is the shrine. Archeologists call such propaganda centers 'Mussolini museums', a term applicable beyond fascist Italy.

Those who now object to displaying Indian specimens with flora & fauna, overlook the fact that natural history museums include all life, no exceptions.

In the late19th century, American museums of natural history were established in New York, Washington, Chicago. By far the most prominent was the American Museum of Natural History (AMNH). Boas urged Heye to merge with it. Nicolas Murray Butler, President of Columbia University, sought a similar merger. Heye rejected both. Then, twenty years after Heye's death, it was reconsidered.

The AMNH, with City & State support, offered land adjoining the AMNH; a $56m wing ($13m City, $13m State, $30m AMNH with endowment); $35m installation; plus $4m a year from the City for maintenance. State & City commitments were published in their annual reports.

Roland Force, Director at the MAI, wanted no part of it. In negotiations, he made no effort to conceal his hostility toward the Director, Thomas Nicholson, or its President, Robert Goelet. He insisted on merging as equals. There was nothing equal about them. One was world famous; the other, a bankrupt disaster. The whole point of these negotiations was to save what still remained of the MAI collection & to do so legally, publicly.

Charles Simon, MAI trustee & investment manager at Salomon Brothers, asked a Texan to help the MAI find a new home. In 1985, he came to New York, visited the Museum, Annex, & gold collection, then met with trustees selected by Barber Conable. Conable, a Republican Congressman, was Chairman of the MAI Board.

To handle public relations, Simon hired ██████ ████████████, America's most successful public relations firm. An article promoting this Texas proposal soon appeared in ██████ magazine (partly owned by ████████████); next, an article in *Connaissance*; then. . . .

The Texan wrote to the MAI Board, offering to raise $70 million & move the museum to Texas. His letter avoided specifics. These came later. ██████ & ████████████ Corporation jointly owned a large tract of land between Fort Worth & Dallas. In the 1980s, they planned a cargo airport there, to be run by ████ ██████, Junior. On adjoining land, they envisioned an outdoor/indoor theme park featuring Patriotism. Indians, somehow, were part of this.

Each partner offered $35m, specifying that donations be tax-deductible. Since $70 million exceeded the MAI endowment, this required re-chartering. A majority of new trustees would be Texans. Among other things, this offered ██████ & ████████████ at least the potential to control their tax-free, $70m contribution. Yet Heye's Deed of Trust left this collection to the People of the State of New York, to be housed in a museum located in New York City, its trustees to meet there at least three times a year & report annually to the State. It could not be more explicit.

The MAI Board appointed a committee of three Trustees to examine the matter. All were lawyers familiar with trusts. All reported the Trust was too tightly written. In open court, it would be 'thrown out . . . the Judge would laugh.'

Acting counsel suggested a surrogate might be more approachable than a judge. This wasn't pursued.

CASH?

Barber Conable, now Chairman of the Board, told me, by phone, that the Texan was sending, in addition to the $70m, what he called 'advance funds.' He called these 'substantial' & said it would be 'useless for me to oppose the offer', or some such phrase.

At the next Board meeting, trustees discussed how these 'advance funds' might be spent. Suggestions of bribery named names: 'He can be had! He can be had!'; 'We have a contact there' [with that office]; etc.

That meeting turned me from supporter to critic. I returned to my office & typed out a detailed account. I showed this to an attorney. He insisted I accompany him to the local U.S. Attorney General's office. FBI agents there already knew far more than I. They asked me to 'go wired' to the next Board meeting. I declined.

I next met with Robert Abrams, again accompanied by counsel. By then, the Texas proposal was stone dead. William Weld, then an Assistant Attorney General, later Governor of Massachusetts, learned of it through his sister-in-law, Dr. Anna Roosevelt, an MAI Curator. Weld went directly to Robert Abrams, twice. A story appeared in *New York Magazine*. Roosevelt was immediately fired.[1]

The New York Times remained sympathetic to the MAI remaining in New York. I was interviewed about the previous Board meeting. I spoke openly. The moment that article appeared, a recent trustee, ████ ████, phoned, furious: 'Breach of honor . . . unheard of! . . . loyalty.' I said bribery was more than a breach of honor. She didn't deny what had been discussed at the previous Board meeting, but professed 'misunderstanding.'[2]

That 'misunderstood' Board consisted of lawyers, bankers, a Rhodes Scholar, historian, Congressman. Six anthropologists then served: Abrams, Carpenter, Eggan, Fenton, Stone, Sturtevant. Every trustee knew the nature of the Texas proposal. No one misunderstood.

There are two kinds of professionals: those with honor ('Show me a hero and I'll show you a corpse') & those without. Only three objected: William C. Sturtevant, a Smithsonian ethnologist; H. Peter Kriendler, 21 Club partner; & me.[3] Why only three? I can only surmise. Two Trustees had self-interests. For most, however, the Texas proposal cut through the MAI's financial problems. But beneath this lay something else: a disturbing fascination, exhilaration, with power, or proximity to power. After the meeting, a retired museum director said to Charles Simon, 'I've never seen you so lively.' Simon replied: 'I'm turned on by ████ ████.'

The man who 'turned on' Charles Simon was a certifiable fruitcake, known to Texans as 'Mr. Fix.' In ████████ ████████ vs. ████, the court accepted evidence of undue influence on elected & appointed officials in eleven States. Texas has no law prohibiting bribery.

In spite of 500 years of Indian rip-off, many trustees found the opportunity for greed or power irresistible, including Indian trustees.

At Board meetings, the word 'collector' was regularly used in a derogatory sense, overlooking the fact that anthropologists on the MAI Board were paid to do just that. Each drew his or her salary to assemble data, including artifacts. And guard them.

The only member of the Board, known to me, who collected as an investment & sold for profit, including a Washington Peace Medal ($54,000, Sotheby's), looted from the grave of Tisomingo, famed Chickasaw chief, was Barber Conable, Chairman of the MAI Board.[4]

Newspapers gave widespread coverage to MAI losses. The American Anthropological Association remained silent. So did the American Association of Museums (AAM). In 1969, that organization sent an 'investigating' committee to the MAI for Accreditation. Finding little amiss, they granted it. But, when the Trustees finally acted responsibly, dismissing Dockstader for cause, the AAM canceled Accreditation.

COUNSEL

Court proceedings followed. In these proceedings, ███████ ██████████ was identified as counsel for the Board. He was not. At no meeting of the Board or Executive Committee was he appointed counsel. 'We', writes Force, 'had settled on [him] to represent the Museum.'[5] A majority of trustees approved his role, but never officially appointed him to it or paid him. He was paid by a single trustee, through a private foundation. Trustees, personally liable for misuse of Heye Foundation funds, chose to avoid accountability.[6]

Force continued to oppose the MAI joining the AMNH. Donald Oresman, then Chairman, MAI, favored joining. So did his successor, Barber Conable. Conable even threatened to resign if they didn't join. Then the Texas proposal came along & later the New York one.

VOTE

At the next Board meeting, I learned in advance that the State Attorney General sent a telegram to the Board, asking the Board to meet with him before voting on the Texas proposal. I asked Barber Conable if he'd received such a telegram. He said, 'No', and proceeded with the vote.

After the vote, I pressed him again about the telegram. He conceded he'd received a communication from Abrams, but said it was addressed to him personally. I asked if it was addressed to the Chairman of the Board. He took the telegram from his pocket, examined it & admitted it was. At my request, he read it aloud.

I asked him why he hadn't first read it to the Board. Vine Deloria, a lawyer, interrupted to say, 'He just did.' General laughter.

In the end, none of this mattered. The day, the moment, Judge Martin B. Stecher ordered the Texan deposed, he withdrew. Waiting patiently, out of sight, was someone possessing the power to summon & the power to anoint.

Wampum Belts

In prehistoric America, shells from the coast, taken inland by Indian traders, were prized, 'esteemed' might be the right word.

Wampum beads, however, were different. Most were made by colonists with metal drills & lathes. Production centered on Long Island & Chesapeake Bay. From there, wampum was taken inland & it soon became legal tender between tribes. It also served this purpose for colonists on the frontier.

Tribal production was limited. The Adams site, a Seneca village (1570-1590) in western New York, yielded metal-drilled beads-in-progress & marine debitage.[1] Yet, Colonial production dominated. By 1640, one Seneca site alone contained an estimated 250,000 wampum beads. During the Beaver Wars, wampum surged. After 1687 (Denonville), it ceased to be frontier wealth, but took on symbolic meanings as condolence strings, treaty belts, etc.

George Hamell writes: 'Wampum was sorted and strung at the Albany Almshouse, associated with the Dutch Reformed Church. From mid-17th century through the early 18th century, the Church placed collection boxes for the poor throughout Albany. Given the scarcity of coinage and the availability of wampum, most donated wampum for the poorhouse. There it was sorted into "good" and "inferior" wampum, the latter probably inferior in size, proportion, finish, color or broken.

'Most poorhouse income was wampum. Coins were few. Needy residents received wampum as loans or gifts. It paid for nursing and medicine. It might even be used to ransom a child from Indians. And it was sold to fur traders.'[2]

Many 17th century ball-headed war clubs were inlaid with wampum beads, often as vertebrae, the club itself being conceived as anthropomorphic.

From 1640-1687, wampum played two roles: as personal wealth (belts might accompany the dead, especially beloved children) later, as treaty diplomacy. Western representatives passed belts 'across the fire' to indigenous nations & vice versa. Tribal belts were displayed in Johnson Hall & elsewhere. Indigenous nations who received them asked chiefs to interpret & guard them. The French, lacking access to shell, might re-string them.

'After the American War of Independence, the survivors of the Six Nations raked up their council fire on Buffalo Creek and divided the treasury of wampums.'[3] In 1784, Loyalist chiefs moved to the Grand River & rekindled the League fire. They took with them those belts most useful in dealing with the British.

Two sets of belts went to the Grand River. Chief John Skanawati Buck held one set for the 'Elder Brothers': Onondagas, Mohawks, Senecas. James Jamieson held those for the 'Younger Brothers': Cayugas & Oneidas. Today, separate sets of condolence strings, one for each side of the fire, mark this division.

John Buck gave Harriet Maxwell Converse, an author sympathetic to the Iroquois, the Women's Confirmation belt & the Huron Alliance belt. He had no right to do so. They belonged to the Confederacy. She, in turn, gave both to the New York State Museum. When Buck died, 1893, his children sold the belts he held. Four went to the Provincial Museum of Ontario. When the Confederacy chiefs learned of this, they refunded the money & brought them home. Pauline Johnson, poet-performer, acquired two or three. She sold one to Heye & gave another to the English romantic painter Frederick Leighton. The rest were scattered to collectors.

James Jamieson, a Cayuga chief, founded the Six Nations Agricultural Society. A prosperous figure on the Grand River Reserve, he offered the Smithsonian a large collection of Indian artifacts for $3000. An anthropologist on the Smithsonian staff, J.N.B. Hewitt, himself Iroquois, judged the price too high. Jamieson didn't want to sell the belts separately. But when Hewitt balked, he did, in 1899, to Thomas Roddy, a dealer in Indian objects.

ALLIANCES

By 1900, wampum was no longer 'the magnet which called the beaver out of the interior forests.'[4] The fur trade disappeared. Wampum no longer served as frontier wealth. Instead, it bound indigenous nations together.

For the Haudenosaunee, the earliest use of wampum had nothing to do with legal tender. The Peacemaker used strings of wampum to condole Hayonwatha over the death of his daughters. This became the ceremony of condolence, still repeated today.[5]

In 1900, Converse alerted the Superintendent at the Brantford Reserve that wampum belts, once entrusted to Chief Buck, were now in the possession of a Mr. T.R. Roddy, 271 Wabash Ave., Chicago, Ill.'[6]

Civil servants wrote to civil servants. For nine years, nothing happened. Finally, the Secretary of Indian Affairs wrote directly to Roddy. No reply. Roddy had tried, for 11 years, to unload the belts. Finally, 1911, the Indian Exhibits Company had a potential buyer (Heye). They asked Roddy about title. He answered:

> 'I have just returned from the Grand River Reservation Canada, where I spent some time. I found no one who claimed any ownership to my Belts. They have been in the Jamieson family at least 50 years, & are the property of Jos. Jamieson from whom I purchased them. Clara Jamieson['s] daughter, has a large picture framed & hanging on the wall showing several of my belts in council & worn by the dif [sic] Indians in the picture. Her father, 2 brothers of Mrs. Jamieson & other Indians with their names & in firm ground family & Clara Jamieson when a little girl about 10 years old as she is 35 now – picture was taken 25 years ago. She is to have copy made which I will send to you. . . .'[7]

The Indian Exhibits Company wrote to Roddy about the potential buyer, but said it was 'embarrassing to take a person of wealth to an Ex ofs [Express office] to look at a C.O.D.'[8] However, in 1910, Roddy sold 11 belts to the Indian Exhibits Company for $2000. Heye bought them & displayed them at the University Museum.

Hewitt may have known that belts offered by Jamieson & Buck's children were different belts. Others, however, did not. Frank Speck & Edward Sapir then worked for Heye. Both believed the Roddy belts came from Buck's children. In 1914, Sapir, now an anthropologist in Ottawa, wrote to Duncan Scott, Deputy Superintendent, Indian Affairs, advising him that 'missing' belts were displayed in Heye's collection. Speck had identified them, but, Sapir added, Speck 'might find it personally inconvenient' to be the source.'[9]

Duncan Scott, at Sapir's suggestion, wrote to Heye, June 11, 1910. George Pepper replied: Heye would return August first. In October, Scott wrote again, then added: '. . . otherwise I will feel constrained to place this matter in the hands of the Department of Justice for advice.'[10]

Heye replied: 'Upon my return to New York this fall, Mr. Pepper told me of your letter. . . . this letter was destroyed with much of my other mail by fire . . . [I read Scott's June 11 letter in the MAI Archives] . . . judge of my surprise on receiving your extremely discourteous letter of October 3rd . . . I am only too glad to give this information when asked for it . . . in a gentlemanly manner . . . your threat of putting . . . [this] in the hands of your department of justice for advice, does not interest me in the least. . . .'[11]

A week later, Heye advised Scott that his belts all came from a 'reservation of N. Y. State . . . the late Mrs. Converse . . . Oklahoma . . . dealers . . . none catalogued as being Canadian.'[12] Next month, however, he admitted to Scott he purchased the belts from the Benham Indian Trading Company (Indian Exhibits Company?).[13]

Roddy went unmentioned in Heye's letter to Scott, but Heye wrote to Roddy that day: 'You may remember I bought these belts from you through the [Indian Exhibits Company] . . . [can you tell me] how they came into your possession . . . Mr. Scott's letters are rather abrupt in tone and . . . he has intimated he will bring legal proceedings against me.'[14]

EVIDENCE

Without evidence of theft, Heye declined to return the belts. Scott asked the Six Nations chiefs for an affidavit: were the belts national or personal?

The Chiefs provided sufficient information to identify them as stolen. Moreover, they were never informed where the belts were. They also sought to deal with John Buck's children, internally. But by 1924, none of this mattered. Canada tried to seize the existing belts from the Confederacy Chiefs, whom Duncan Scott now sought to remove.[15]

Over 50 years of silence followed. Then, in 1977, Paul Williams, Director, Treaty Research Program, Union of Ontario Indians, Toronto, wrote to the MAI, asking about wampum generally & an Ojibway belt specifically. The reply, by James O'Rorke, essentially refused all information, but said Dr. William Fenton, a Board member, would look into the matter. Fenton's 1977 report to the Chairman of the Board (but not to the board), admitted 'dubious circumstances' surrounding the belts, but nevertheless recommended selling them to Canada for $225,000. Canadian funds were then available.[16]

Williams asked for their return. By 1981, he'd assembled much data, including a copy of the proposed sale. Most trustees knew nothing of this. All sales had been banned, as of 6.29.77. I'd like to think at least some trustees were embarrassed.

In 1986, the MAI Board met with the Six Nations chiefs in New York. Ethics & goodwill prevailed. The belts were returned, 1988. In describing this event, Fenton cast his role as advocate, hardly the case. Moreover, these weren't the belts he presumed them to be. Dr. Elisabeth Tooker compared century-old photographs of the belts. Roddy bought six from James Jamieson & five from persons unknown.[17] Neither Jamieson, nor Buck's children, had the right to sell. Title belonged to the Confederacy.

CHAPTER 4 Invincible

An old friend, a professional photographer, described to me a day he'd spent photographing ███████ ███████████████ in his office. What he remembered most was the ease with which the secretary reached anyone by phone, no matter how powerful, how famous. It was like 'the White House calling' or, more appropriately, like 'Buckingham Palace calling.'

Few delays followed. ████████████████ quietly advocated his cause. He advised who had leverage & how it might be exploited. Public matters were handled privately, confidentially. Senator Daniel K. Inoyue went to that office. He had just introduced a Congressional bill for the Smithsonian to take over the MAI. So did Robert Abrams, New York State's Attorney General. Abrams had been summoned to support that bill.

████████████████ had the power to summon & the power to anoint. At a banquet, he offered Barber Conable the Presidency of the World Bank. *The New York Times* obituary of Conable, 2003, called his appointment 'surprising' since he had 'no specific expertise in banking, especially on an international level, or wide experience in management.'[1] But he was Chairman of the MAI Board.

BATTERY PARK

Battery Park used land-fill from the World Trade Center to extend Lower Manhattan. ████████████████'s bank financed this effort. The city added schools, library, etc. He looked for a museum, again at no expense to his bank. The beleaguered Museum of the American Indian qualified.

███████ ███████████████ first encountered Indians in the Southwest Desert. He was then eight: 'On my family's 1926 trip we traveled in a private Pullman railway car accompanied by a doctor and French tutor. Our car was coupled to regularly scheduled trains but would be left off for a few days at a time at sidings along the way so that we could visit points of interest by automobile.'[2]

In Santa Fe, they visited the Museum of New Mexico (which his father supported), the Palaces of the Governors, then various pueblos. At one, San Ildefonso, they met Maria Martinez, the famous potter. The next year, his future wife, ██████, with her parents, also visited Maria.

██████████'s parents bought local art, especially the work of E. Irving Couse (18 pictures), plus Indian souvenirs. These ended up in a 'rest house', adjoining the main summer home in Maine. Decorated in Desert Style, it displayed Navaho blankets, rugs, concho belts, *kachinas*.

RETURN

'In 1974, █████ and I returned together to San Ildefonso [each had gone there independently, years before]. We were delighted to find that Maria Martinez was still alive and well, and that she even remembered our first visits with our families nearly fifty years earlier.

'In October, 1985 . . . I was speaking at a conference on philanthropy in New Orleans. One of the other speakers was my friend Barber Conable . . . I discovered that he was chairman of the board of The Museum of the American Indian and he was concerned about an offer . . . to provide a new home for the museum . . . [in] Dallas. . . . He told me that an effort to [merge the MAI & AMNH] had failed. . . .'

'As it happened, █████ and I had been invited to a small private dinner in Washington. . . . The guests of honor were President and Mrs. Reagan. . . . At the dinner I seized the opportunity to tell the President about the plight of The Museum of the American Indian and to ask him if he would be prepared to take steps to make the Custom House available for the museum. To my delight he expressed great interest in the project and said he would see what could be done. The very next day he initiated action to have the [Custom House] available for use by the Indian museum.'[3]

██████████'s account foreshortens events. By May, 1979, he had already assigned an assistant to maneuver the MAI into the Custom House. By 1986, the Mayor of New York asked his assistance in this matter. He replied: 'based on a call I had a few days ago from Don Regan [Reagan's Chief of Staff], I gather the White House is as interested as ever.' He urged Mayor Koch to talk to Senator D'Amato 'who seems to be willing to withdraw his opposition.'

Later that year he wrote to the Mayor: 'encouraged to learn you will give every consideration to the Custom House offer.' In 1988, he commissioned the Cambridge Report. It recommended that move. By 1989, he was ████████ ██ ███ █████.

In New York State, any trust that moves elsewhere transfers its files to the NYS-AG's office. The last law firm to represent the MAI, was ████ █████, of which ████████████ was a partner. They listed '369 files and boxes', but promised to send them over. Then they refused. A year later, what arrived wasn't '369 files and boxes', but 7 half-filled boxes of mostly printed material. I assume sensitive documents were shredded. As a former trustee, I believe I was entitled to see records for those years. In addition to chance discoveries, the following items caught my eye:

20   Anthropology Collection – survey

23   Bills

40   Client documents – satisfaction of mortgage

43   Collections

49   Correspondence

107   Documents not produced – external correspondence

130   Force deposition note

132   Force mortgage forgiveness

160   Judge Stecher information sheet

166   Legal research – MAI case (motion to dismiss) – AMNH Annual Reports – confidential memo for counsel – Curtis-Mallet and Bishop Museum files – documents produced to AG per subpoena – Carpenter and Johnson files – Conable deposition file – Box 5

276   Stecher conference 2/17/89 (not accessible to me)

315   Working file – letter from Huerta

THE COURT

When Judge Martin B. Stecher ruled that the Texan be deposed, the Texan immediately withdrew his 'offer.' The press never asked 'Why?'

Surely this required a tight, thoroughly coordinated public relations campaign, worthy of the firm that was hired.

According to Court transcript, 13 January 1987, Judge Martin B. Stecher stated: 'Let us take the scenario that the [MAI] museum trustees, the plaintiffs in this action, were totally unreasonable, which is entirely possible in dealing with the American Museum of Natural History.' As a witness to those negotiations ('dealing' to Judge Stecher), I felt the AMNH acted with honor, the MAI did not.

Judge Stecher also ruled that the Huntington Free Library (HFL) belonged to the Smithsonian. He called defense claims 'meritless.' The Appellate Court disagreed. They said the Huntington Free Library belonged to the People of the State of New York.

███████ █████

In 1986, Barber Conable became President, World Bank.[1] █████ █████, a recent Board member, took over the MAI Board. According to Curt Muser, her foundation, the ██████████ █. ████████ ███████████, put $3.5 million into the MAI. They paid the salaries of █████████, █████, ████, others. Later she donated over $3 million to the NMAI, specifying that a hall be named for Roland Force.

CUSTOM HOUSE

In 1985, Barber Conable arranged for a TV special, funded by the Xerox Corporation. When it was released, 1987, it achieved national coverage. Nearly 400 licensed public stations screened it. Many individuals were interviewed, including Conable from his World Bank office.

Initially, ██████████ hoped the MAI would occupy the entire Custom House. Finances reduced this to the ground floor for displays, the second floor for offices & library. The remaining building went to the Bankruptcy Court.

Constructed in 1899, it's a magnificent building, well worth preserving, but not as a museum. Roughly 40% is devoted to walls, corridors, stairwells, elevators. A railway track once delivered coal to the basement. The display area is donut-shaped. Moreover, New York already had a museum with major Indian exhibits.

Robert McCormack Adams, then Secretary of the Smithsonian, proposed that the MAI & AMNH Indian collections be joined by computer. United, they'd be unparalleled. Touring shows could be mounted to display on the Mall, in Washington, or the AMNH, in New York, then tour.

What Adams didn't anticipate was the rage of those promoting the Custom House. This wasn't what *they* had decided. A 'stunned' █████ ████ 'vociferously stated she knew nothing about the matter.' Within minutes, she called 'counsel' who 'was outraged.'[4] Yet Adams' suggestion had great merit. A 72-page *Agreement* between City/State & Smithsonian blocks that sensible approach.[5]

Until he went to college, George Heye's mother *&* nurse called him 'Baby George.' In 1947, age 73, after 'negotiations for yet another fine stash of Indian material', he wrote, 'Me happy boy.'

He assembled great treasures, but as private possessions, to do with as he liked. He discarded field notes *&* maps, dumped potsherds, falsified records. He thereby wiped out significant moments in Indian history. No scholar tolerated him for long. He relaxed with those who found his antics amusing.

Yet, compared to his successors, his secrecy was childlike. The MAI, under Dockstader, can only be described as sick. And, for all of their charm — and both were very charming — Curt Muser *&* Roland Force reveled in secrecy. Inventory results were concealed from the Board *&* funding source. So was much else.

If the New York press had printed the AMNH offer or the details of the Texas proposal, would the Heye trust have been trashed? We'll never know. Letters to the *Times* were submitted by Robert Goelet, President, AMNH; Donald Oresman, Chairman of the Board, MAI; *&* me. They never appeared.

The *Times* went further. I submitted an OpEd piece. It was initially accepted. Then an editor called to say it wouldn't run. Later I pointed out errors in a 4.14.85 article, Week in Review. These went uncorrected. Congressman Ted Weiss asked why? I said I didn't know.

Douglas C. McGill, a *Times* reporter for Cultural Affairs, wrote most of these articles. He never mentioned the Texas plans for an amusement park (patriotism; cowboys *&* Indians), though the Dallas press carried details. Nor did he mention that ▪▪▪▪▪ jointly owned land with ▪▪▪▪▪▪▪▪▪▪ Corporation where all this would occur.

McGill *&* I lunched together twice. I remember dropping off, at his office, the State *&* City commitments to the AMNH, published in their annual reports. No word of this appeared in the *Times*. When I last saw McGill, he told me he had just resigned over censorship. I don't know if this was true or not, but, if so, it was belated.

Barber Conable was said to be a good friend of the Editor of the *Times*. But clearly there was something more. A new Assistant Director, MAI, was brought in. He lacked museum experience *&* anthropological training, but had an uncle, a senior editor at the *Times*.

Secrecy under Heye got worse under Dockstader *&* continued after 1977 for other reasons. Force denied all responsibility for the inventory, which took four years, though he was Director during most of that time. In negotiating with the Lilly Foundation about moving the MAI to Indianapolis, he recommended the move, after accepting a 'consultant fee.' At the time of the Texan's proposal, trustee Charles Simon, who first approached the Texan, gave Force a new Mercedes. His mortgage on a hill-top home, Oahu, was forgiven. He was paid to write *The Heye & the Mighty*.[6] Its printing was subsidized.

THE HEYE & THE MIGHTY

The University of Oklahoma Press initially accepted the Force manuscript. I saw a copy & wrote to the editor of inaccuracies. He asked if he might forward my letter to Force. I urged him to do so. Before my comments reached Force, he died. The publisher canceled publication.

The book appeared four years later, subsidized by Charles Simon. Before printing, it was greatly enlarged & sharply edited. The editors, unaware that Force never saw my letter to the Oklahoma Press, had him respond in the first person singular, thus offering evidence — of a sort — of life transcending death.

The Heye & the Mighty isn't the story of the breaking of a trust. Nor does it describe the MAI collection, about which most trustees revealed vast ignorance. It's a tale in which that collection never serves as an object of contention, but the occasion of a moral drama. The hero, Force, tempered & tested by training, departs paradise & arrives in Gotham, center of violence, filth, treachery, but also of hidden treasures (Custom House) & modest saints (Julie Kidd). In this citadel of the 'mighty', our hero, predestined to play a forceful role among giants & to lead 'a remarkable crusade', suffers, endures, survives. 'To strive, to seek, to find, but not to yield.' Sinners fail, saints 'prevail.' 'A wonderful season follows '[7]

EVALUATING THE MAI

I met George Heye only once, casually, pleasantly. My evaluation of his museum was never personal. It was professional. So is my evaluation of Roland Force & most of the MAI trustees. They used that collection for their own ends & egos. Most trustees couldn't tell a microlith from a megalith. Case 73 at the MAI displayed a classic Maori whalebone club, *wahaika*, from New Zealand, here identified as coming from California — a form familiar to any anthro major. Certainly it must have been familiar to Force, a former Curator of Oceanic Cultures. Yet, in 17 years in that tiny museum, Force never noticed or never bothered.[8]

Heye's museum was flawed from the beginning. It got steadily worse. A few trustees sought to preserve its collection. They opposed those eager to sell it or those enamored with their trustee role. Whatever the Smithsonian may have promised the Director & trustees about their continued presence, it didn't work out that way. Both suddenly found themselves 'outside', looking in at a collection they never knew.

EVALUATING THE NMAI

What impresses me most about the NMAI is its openness. Secrecy no longer prevails. The difference is overwhelming. The new staff knows little of the past or finds it mildly amusing. Just as well.

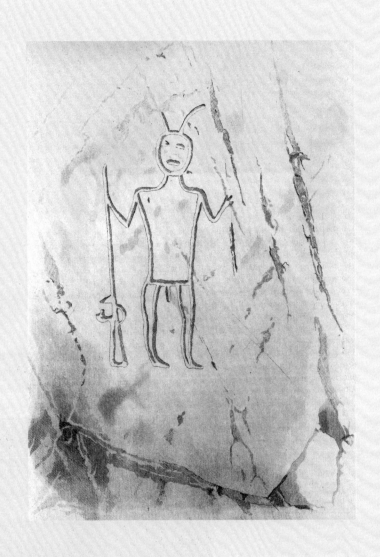

Petroglyph

I'm indebted to George Hamell, New York State Museum, Albany, for a remarkable document, dated 1712. It describes the intended distribution of 12 framed & 192 unframed prints of the four Iroquois who visited England in 1710, known as the 'Four Kings of Canada.' One framed print was assigned 'to the 5 Nations to be placed in ye Onondagas Castle where the 5 nations meet.' Unframed prints were assigned to 'Each of ye 5 nations & ye River Indians' & 'to ye 4 Indians who went to England.'

NOBLE HUNTER

One of these prints shows Sa Ga Yeath Qua Pieth Tow, 'King of the Maquas' [Mohawks], also known as Brant, in classic European posture: lord of the manor, gentleman hunter, Indian chief.

Ideally, this posture shows the right foot forward. The raised right hand grasps the barrel of a grounded musket & the left hand points down. A dog, opposite the musket, joins the hunter. Here a bear substitutes for the dog.

It's a noble pose. Emperor Charles V (1500–1558) presented himself to posterity in precisely this manner. So did other nobles. This classic posture of divine nobility requires that the right foot be forward, the right hand

pointing toward the upper world, the left hand pointing to the lower world & the body aligned to the *axis mundi*. When seated, the figure holds a scepter in the right hand, symbolizing the *axis mundi* as the climbing pole.

Whirling Dervishes are even more explicit: right hand up, left hand down, body as *axis mundi*, with cap & gown symbolizing the sky dome in planetary rotation. In the European Renaissance this symbolism became less explicit yet basically survived. Each of the Four Kings of Canada was painted in this posture. That posture was reserved for divine royalty. English military negotiated with Indian chiefs on a one-to-one basis.

European visitors to America, after returning home, loved to strike this pose, bedecked in Indian garb, standing for portraits against a forest background. This is how we remember Meriwether Lewis, from an 1807 watercolor.

That same posture served as a model for Indians themselves. George Catlin made his 1838 portrait of Osceola, a Seminole chief, from life. It shows Osceola, who was left-handed, grasping his grounded musket in his outstretched left hand. An Ottawa mission-school artist later embroidered that portrait in leather, presumably from Catlin's lithograph. Full circle is achieved in *A Pictorial History of Costume* (Bruhn & Tilke, 1973:199), which offers Osceola's pose as typically American Indian.

ESOPUS PETROGLYPH

In 1853, Henry R. Schoolcraft published a hand-tinted, full-page illustration of a petroglyph chiseled at Esopus Landing, on the west side of the Hudson River, New York. True, both hands are raised. It also lacks a dog. Otherwise, it conforms to the European format: lord of the manor, gentleman hunter, Indian chief.

It's now underwater. The repatriation law, NAGPRA, means the National Museum of the American Indian owns it. I wrote to the Director there, offering to provide Rock Foundation funds to recover it & place it in Washington, at the new museum on the Mall. I received no answer.

The dead can't sue for libel. The living can. Where appropriate, their names have been deleted in the manner of the Freedom of Information Act.

CHAPTER 1:

1/ Mason, 1958.

2/ Burnett, 1964, NMAI, VW, 13.

3/ Wallace, 1960.

4/ Bird, 1960:10.

5/ Bird, 1960:10-11.

6/ Bird, 1960:11.

7/ Mason, 1958:10.

8/ Wallace, 1960:14-15.

9/ Wallace, 1960:15-16.

10/ Mason, 1958:11.

11/ Saville, 1910.

12/ Anthropology Archives, AMNH, 1905.

13/ In 1910, Clark Wissler wrote to P.E. Goddard, then both at the AMNH, 'Saville was cut off the list at the recent meeting of the [AMNH] executive meeting for sufficient reasons – that is, he resigned. Mr. Heye now has no representation on our staff to complicate matters, National Anthropological Archives, Smithsonian Institution.

14/ King & Little, 1986.

15/ *The New York Times*, 5 Oct 1913:II.6.

16/ Heye & Pepper, 1915.

17/ Lothrop (Samuel), 1957.

18/ King & Little, 1986:44.

19/ King & Little, 1986:45.

20/ Burnett, 1964:17.

21/ Culin, 1901:144-145.

22/ Culin, 1905:52; the NMAI retains many Tozier pieces. A later collection, assembled by Tozier, is now at the Oakland City Museum, Oakland, California.

23/ Culin, 1908:77.

24/ NMAI:VX:15.

25/ NMAI:VX:15.

26/ Bird, 1960:15.

27/ Bird, 1960:8. As a boy, Heye did collect stamps. After 1897, he sold his collection for $20K, then an enormous sum.

28/ Bird, 1960:8.

29/ Mason, 1958:21.

30/ Wallace, 1960:26.

31/ Anthropology Archives, AMNH.

32/ Bird, 1960:12-13.

SHRUNKEN MEN:

1/ Saville,1929.

2/ A. Hyatt Verrill tells of one other entire body in his autobiography, ms. 383. NMAI Archives.

3/ Letter from F. K. Seward to Frederick C. Harding, 25.8.23, NMAI Archives.

4/ Sworn affidavit of Patrick J. Cherry, 25.8.23, NMAI Archives.

5/ Letter from C.M. Larrea, Lima, 3.9.23, quoted in letter to F.K. Seward, Secretary, Heye Board, from Marshall H. Saville, 4.9.23, NMAI Archives.

6/ Duncan, 2000:145-147.

7/ Alexander, 1994:179.

CHAPTER 2:

1/ Burnett, 1964:4.

2/ Burnett, 1964:7.

3/ Krech, 1994:12.

4/ Gibson, 1980:9-24.

5/ Burnett, 1964:7.

6/ Wallace, 1960:26.

7/ Wallace, 1960:26.

8/ A. Hyatt Verrill, Archives, NMAI.

9/ Abrams, 1994:xiii-xiv.

10/ Heye letter to Plecker, NMAI Archives, OC 236.

SACRED MAT:

1/ Girouard, 1984:175.

2/ Hall (Courtney), 1934.

3/ King, 1994:115.

5/ Mitchell, 1817.

6/ King, 1994:60.

7/ Schuster, 1986, 3/1:28-35.

CHAPTER 3:

1/ Bird, 1960:9.

2/ Burnett, 1964:15.

3/ Burnett, 1964:24.

4/ Burnett, 1964:25. See Shoemaker, 1999 & Wierzbowski, 1999.

5/ Burnett, 1964:24-26.

6/ Burnett, 1964:25-26.

7/ Myers, 1984.

8/ Barnhart, 1998:136-137. Not the present American Anthropological Association.

9/ Charles F. Wray series, plus various Proceedings, Rochester Museum & Science Center.

10/ Dundar, 1962.

11/ Lenz, 2004.

12/ Burnett, 1964:18.

13/ Personal communication, 8.8.04, Michael Cowdrey, POB 1630, San Luis Obispo, CA. About 80% of this ms. has been printed, under other names: Ewers, 1959 & 1960; as well as Nabokov, 1967. The remainder consists of myths & songs.

14/ Mason, 1958:23.

15/ Burnett, 1964.

16/ Burnett, 1964.

17/ Court order & lawyer's letter, NMAI Archives.

18/ Smith (J.G.E.), 1980.

19/ Davis, 1991.

20/ Burnett, 1964:14-15.

ESKIMO MAP:

1/ Speck, 1924:143-149.

2/ Tremblay, 1921.

3/ Noah Piugaattuk, 1994, tape IE-303, Oral History Project, Igloolik Research Centre.

4/ Hall (Charles), 1879.

5/ Rosie Igallijuq, 1991, tape IF-204, Oral History Project, Igloolik Research Centre.

6/ *Ibid.*

7/ Noah Piugaattuk, 1989, tape IE-041, Oral History Project, Igloolik Reseach Centre.

8/ Bernier, 1939:379-381; Grant, 2005.

9/ Noah Piugaattuk, 1989, *op.cit.*

10/ *Ibid.*

11/ Fortunately, Speck, 1924, published the account of the man marooned.

CHAPTER 4:

1/ Amos Oneroad was driving. The car slid down an embankment, pinning Skinner beneath it.

2/ Wallace, 1960:6.

3/ NMAI Archives, 4.16.26.

4/ Fienup-Riordan, 1996:251.

5/ Fienup-Riordan, 1996.251.

6/ Fienup-Riordan, 1996:251.

7/ Fienup-Riordan, 1996:175.

8/ Fienup-Riordan, 1996:175.

9/ Fienup-Riordan, 1996:257.

10/ Speck, 1928.

11/ Prince & Speck, 1904.

12/ Library, University of Pennsylvania, Philadelphia.

13/ Hallowell, 1926. Speck began this study, then turned it over to Hallowell. When Hallowell delayed publishing, Speck warned he'd bring it out under his own name if further delays followed. Hallowell collected 9 scrolls, which he sold to Heye in 1932 for $865.

14/ Davidson, 1937.

15/ NMAI computer check, 3.3.05.

16/ Dundar, 1962.

17/ Lenz, 2004:title.

18/ Smith (J.G.E.), 1980.

19/ Davis, 1991..

20/ Burnett 1964:18.

21/ Brown (Alison K.), 1998 & 2001.

22/ Dr. Alison K. Brown, Glasgow Museum, personal communications, 25.11.98 & 21.01.99.

23/ Cadzow earlier collected for Heye among the Ojibwa. See Cadzow, 1926.

24/ At some point, the expedition collected two Midé scrolls, listed in Dewdney, 1975:190.

25/ Cadzow, 1929.

CHAMPLAIN SITE:

1/ Carpenter, 1956:90.

2/ Loring, 1985:101.

3/ Stephen Loring, personal communication, 2.25.04.

4/ Loring, 1985:98.

5/ In 1937, Olsen surveyed sites along the Bruneau River, Idaho. Louis Schellbach also worked in Idaho in 1930. Their reports, prepared for publication, went unpublished or under later names.

CHAPTER 5:

1/ NMAI Archives, Box OC 121:1-4.

2/ Bird, 1960:8.

3/ Wardle, 1929:121.

4/ Wardle, 1929:119.

5/ Davis, 1987:25 (Moore's collection).

6/ Smith (Murphy), 1997.

7/ Wardle, 1929:120.

8/ Wardle, 1929:121.

9/ George Heye to Clarence B. Moore, 5.9.29, NMAI Archives.

10/ Wardle, 1929:121.

11/ NMAI Archives, Heye letter to Moore, 1929.

12/ NMAI Archives, Heye letter to Moore (cont.), 1929.

13/ Stein, 1993:112.

14/ Wardle, 1929:121.

15/ Burnett, 1964:17.

17TH CENTURY CLUB:

1/ Leach, 1958:200-204; Bodge, 1906:242-249.

2/ Schuster & Carpenter, 1996:79-129.

3/ Archives nationales, Paris, Colonies C11A(2) f. 268. Rendering by O'Callaghan, DocRelColHistNY, v:9, 1855:50; corrected by William Sturtevant. Multiple sources: Lafitau, 1724, 2:43; Jordan, 1909; Journal of Adam Hubley, MS Am643, 1779 & MS Vi 1411.Q.3a, Original Journals & Extracts [Sullivan raid], Du Simitiere coll., Historical Society of Pennsylvania, Philadelphia. Pictographic system analyzed by William Sturtevant, George Hamell & particularly Scott Meachum, Hudsonville, Michigan, an independent scholar who, more than anyone else, broke this iconographic code.

4/ Archives nationales, Paris: Colonies C11A2 f. 268.

5/ Hamell, 1979.

6/ John King was a common name in the Massachusetts Colony: Bodge, 1906, cites the 1675-76 enlistments of several. One, however, is identified as, 'King, John, North[hampton].' 'Medad King, N'hamton, son of John King,' is later listed as eligible for a land grant for his father's service on that occasion.

7/ According to family history, the club went from Lt. John King to his son, Medad (b. 1699; then to Medad's son, Medad II (b. 1730); next to Medad II's son, Thaddeus (1760-1782). At some point, the club was transferred to descendants of King's daughter, Experience. Experience King married Col. Timothy Dwight. Their grandson, the Rev. Dr. Timothy Dwight (1758-1817), President of Yale University, wrote of local Indians: 'Another of their principal weapons was the well-known Tomahawk, or war-club. I had one of these in my possession many years; in shape, not unlike a Turkish sabre, but much shorter, and more clumsy. On it were formed several figures of men, by putting thin strips of copper, set edge-wise in the wood. Some of them were standing; some were prostrate; and a few had lost their heads. The last two were supposed to denote the number of enemies, whom the owner of the Tomahawk professed himself to have killed.' His memory wasn't perfect, but no question: it's the same club: Dwight, 1810, 1:118.

The last family owner, Mrs. Esther Diefendorf, was the daughter of Florence Irene Bates Johnson, a descendant of Experience King. In the 1970s, she lent the club to the MAI. As family records go, this documentation is exceptionally good, though it should be used with caution. We know only that: John King was at the Falls Fight; the club fits that period; it entered the King family at an early date.

CHAPTER 6:

1/ King & Little, 1986:44.

2/ Heye to Daniel Wolf, Elbowoods, North Dakota, 3.nd.35, NMAI Archives, Box VT:4.

3/ Wallace, 1960:26-27.

4/ Wallace, 1960:27-28.

5/ Burnett, 1964:18-19.

6/ Smith (Watson) et al., 1966.

7/ Mason, 1958:28.

8/ Married: 6.25.36.

9/ Wallace, 1960:28.

10/ Burnett, 1964:23.

11/ Bird, 1960:7-8.

12/ Junius Bird, Anthropology Archives, AMNH, New York.

13/ Lothrop (Samuel), 1957:66-67.

14/ Letter from Hodge to Heye & Heye's reply, Anthropology Archives, Southwest Museum, Los Angeles.

18TH CENTURY CLUB:

1/ Burch, 1990:261-282.

2/ Burch, 1990:266 & 273.

3/ Stone, 1865, 2:210.

4/ George Wray document, 1771, Rock Foundation, New York.

5/ Lender & Martin, 1982:49-54.

6/ 'Proceedings of a General Court Martial at German Flats on July 29, 1776,' Papers of the Third New Jersey Regiment, New York State Library, Misc. papers. Albany.

7/ George Clinton to Pierre du Simitiere, 3.27.79, *The Public Papers of George Clinton*, 10 vols, New York & Albany, 1899-1914, 4:673-74.

8/ Archives nationales, Paris, Colonies C11A2 f. 268.

9/ O'Callaghan, DHSNY, 1850, 1:12.

10/ Extensive personal communication with William Sturtevant.

11/ Stone, 1865, 2:62-63. The use of '8' to represent the 'u' sound was, I'm told, limited to the French.

12/ Phillips & Idiens, 1994:24.

13/ Schellbach, 1928:157-166.

14/ Stone, 1865, 2:62-63.

15/ Corey, 1921-62, 3:630, 747, 751-2, 754, 862; 7:129; 10:895; 11:354; 12:200; 13:111, 168; 16:619-621; *Dictionary of Canadian Biography*, 1979, 4:587-588.

16/ Stone, 1865, 2:62-63.

17/ Schellbach, 1928:160-161.

18/ Gavin K. Watt, Museum of Applied Military History, King City, Ontario, Canada, personal communication, 9.28.98.

19/ Everard, 1891:79.

20/ NMAI Archives, Box OC 239:4.

21/ NMAI Archives, Box OC 239:4.

22/ NMAI Archives, Box OC 239:4.

CHAPTER 7:

1/ NMAI Archives, VT4, condensed & with ampersands.

2/ Pepper & Wilson, 1908.

3/ NMAI Archives, VT4.

4/ Wilson, 1907:52.

5/ Gilman & Schneider, 1987:297.

6/ Wilson, 1906:139, 142-150.

7/ Wilson, 1906:13.

8/ Wilson, 1906:142, 144-145.

9/ Wilson, 1907:6-14; Gilman & Schneider, 1987:296-299.

10/ Gilman & Schneider, 1987:301.

11/ NMAI Archives, VT:4.

12/ NMAI Archives, VT:4.

13/ Gilman & Schneider, 1987:343.

14/ Heye, 11.15.34.

15/ Case, 12.6.34.

16/ Bowers, 12.31.34.

17/ Collier, 1.12.35.

18/ Heye, 1.17.35.

19/ Case, 1.14.35.

20/ Heye, 3.29.35.

21/ Case, 4.6.35.

22/ Beyer, 4.24.35.

23/ Collier, 5.28.35.

24/ Beyer, 7.22.37.

25/ Parks, 1992:xxii.

26/ Case, 7.19.37.

27/ Heye, 12.3.37.

28/ Balsam, 7.19.37.

29/ NMAI Archives, Video.

30/ Myers, 1977:206-208.

31/ Lowie, 1959:104.

32/ Gilbert L. Wilson, 6.14.16, Anthropology Archives, AMNH.

33/ Wilson, 1907

34/ Lévi-Strauss, 1979:288.

MASTERWORK:

1/ Paul Rigg, gun dealer & 'runner' for a Pennsylvania gallery, tried to peddle the lot for $50K. Shortly afterward, he died.

2/ Force suspected Venables of theft & Selser of collusion. Yet they alone acted responsibly. Venables lost his job at the MAI & found no academic employment for six years. He's now at Cornell University. Selser closed his New York gallery & returned to Santa Fe. My wife paid Smith's bill: $18,000.

3/ *The New York Times*, 9.1.82, p. B3.

4/ *The New York Post*, 9.1.82, p. 3.

CHAPTER 8:

1/ Lévi-Strauss, 1943:175-182.

2/ Lévi-Strauss, 1985:261.

3/ Dolores Vanetti, interview, 02.18.05.

4/ Sawin, 1995:185.

5/ Dolores Venetti, interview, 02.18.05.

6/ Lévi-Strauss, 1985:260-261.

7/ Eliza Breton, personal communication, 7.14.70.

8/ Furrier Jacques Kaplan.

9/ Claude Lévi-Strauss, personal communication, 11.17.74.

10/ Sawin, 1995:169.

11/ Fienup-Riordan, 1996:215.

12/ Lévi-Strauss, 1985:243-247.

13/ The Rock Foundation purchased a number of ex-Heye artifacts on the art market. See Holm & Reid, 1975:257, note 12: 'The Museum of the American Indian has declined to make available for this publication either the catalog entries or field notes on these specimens. Perhaps some day the specimens and data can be reunited.'

14/ Curated by Frederic Douglas & René d'Harnoncourt.

15/ Schuster Archives. Museum für Völkerkunde, Basel.

16/ Bird, 1960:7.

17/ Bird, 1960:7 (cont.).

18/ NMAI Archives, Heye to Carlebach, 1953.

FIGURINE:

1/ Carpenter, 1942 & 2002. Initial survey: 1938.

2/ Sempowski & Saunders, 2001:32-36.

NOTES / GREED

CHAPTER 1:

1/ Archives, Nelson-Atkins Museum of Art, Kansas City, 03.15.00.

2/ Hodge letter to Heye, 3.19.32, Archives, Southwest Museum, MS 7:1, 286, Los Angeles.

3/ Heye's reply, 3.23.32, Archives, Southwest Museum, MS 7:1, 286, Los Angeles.

4/ NMAI Registrar, 4.27.04.

5/ Fienup-Riordan, 1996:260.

6/ NMAI Archives, Heye to Dockstader, 1955.

7/ Force, 1995:58. This explains Force's statement, original version of *The Heye & the Mighty*, that the inventory discovered specimens listed as Deaccessioned, which were, in fact, not missing.

8/ Printed, 1978, *Indian Notes*, 12, Museum of the American Indian.

CHRISTIAN CROSS:

1/ Belmont, 1952.

2/ Parker, 1913.

3/ Belmont, 1952:47-48.

4/ Thwaites, 1896-1901, 61:159.

5/ Thwaites, 1896-1901, 6:253.

6/ Thwaites, 1896-1901, 51:129.

7/ Thwaites, 1896-1901, 61:57.

8/ Thwaites, 1896-1901, 11:251; 22:239; 42:135, 147; 54:37, 101, 112.

9/ Belmont, 1952:49.

10/ Belmont, 1952:52.

11/ Belmont, 1952:53-57.

12/ Thwaites, 1896-1901, 22:243.

13/ Thwaites, 1896-1901, 52:125.

14/ Noyan, 1720:75.

15/ Thwaites, 1896-1901, 51:125.

16/ Belmont, 1952:63.

17/ Flick, 1939, 10:629 & 638.

CHAPTER 2:

1/ MAI catalogue: 9/3445.

2/ At the first meeting of the newly-constituted Board, a motion was passed to appoint Lord Day Lord as the new law firm. That same firm, in a 27-page report, defended sales used for operations.

3/ See NMAI Archives, Box FD 029:3, 1974.

4/ Dockstader had a machine making rubber stamps. He used these to 'authorize' exchanges with several galleries. Most were used long after those galleries closed.

5/ Force, 1999:44, listed Rock Foundation funding for the Inventory at $400,000. In fact, it was considerably more. Total commitment to the MAI: $875,000.

6/ Dealers, at least in American Indian material, keep few records. Museums do. A wealth of ex-Heye pieces were found in American & European museums.

7/ Report of Joel Cooper, New York State Assistant Attorney General.

8/ I recall counsel saying, 'I need irrefutable evidence of two examples of illegal dealings, for each of those four', or words to that effect. I provided that.

NAXNÓX:

1/ Dr. Jay Miller quoted in Sotheby's catalog.

2/ Hammer price ($684,500), plus buyer's premium.

CHAPTER 3:

1/ Dr. Anna Roosevelt later won a MacArthur 'genius' Award.

2/ See Force, 1999:255-258, concerning bribery discussed at the 02.22.85 Board meeting. Since this doesn't appear in Force, 1995, presumably it was added.

3/ When *The New York Times* refused to print details of the Texas proposal, my only hope lay in open court. With this in mind, I voted in favor of the Texas proposal. It was a mistake.

4/ Chief Tishomingo fought in the American Revolution beside 'Mad' Anthony Wayne; served in 1812 under Andrew Jackson; fought for the U.S. in nine battles. The Chickasaw protested the desecration of his grave, by a road crew. They asked for the bones, the medal. Instead, it went to someone who, in his own words, called it 'an investment.' Section 1166(b) of NAGPRA provides 'that whoever knowingly sells, purchases, uses for profit, or transports for sale or profit Native American funerary objects, sacred objects or objects of cultural patrimony obtained in violation of the Act shall be subject to a fine or imprisonment not more than 12 months or both.'

5/ ████, ████ ███.

6/ On advice of counsel, I notified MAI trustees, in writing, individually, that, without 'counsel's' signature authorizing the use of Heye funds, trustees could be personally liable for damages.

WAMPUM BELTS:

1/ Ceci, 1986:72.

2/ George Hamell, personal communication, 7.12.99; Fisher, 2003.

3/ Fenton, 1989:401-2.

4/ Weeden, 1884:15.

5/ Paul Williams, personal communication, 3.29.04.

6/ Converse to Cameron, 2.12.10, Williams File, 1979.

7/ Roddy to Indian Exhibits Company, 2.12.10, Williams File, 1979.

8/ Fenton, 1989:405.

9/ Sapir to Scott, 5.16.14, Williams File, 1979.

10/ Scott to Heye, 6.11.14, Williams File, 1979.

11/ Heye to Scott, 10.8.14, Williams File, 1979.

12/ Heye to Scott, 10.15.14, Williams File, 1979.

13/ Heye to Scott, 11.6.14, Williams File, 1979.

14/ Heye to Roddy, 11.6.14, Williams File, 1979.

15/ Paul Williams, personal communication, 3.29.04; Fenton, 1989:407.

16/ Newberry Library, Chicago.

17/ Tooker, 1998:219-236.

CHAPTER 4:

1/ Appointed President, World Bank, 04.15.86.

2/ ██████████, ████:███.

3/ ██████████, ████:███.

4/ ██████, ████:███.

5/ Agreement between and among the City of New York, The State of New York and the Smithsonian Institution with respect to the George Gustav Heye Center of the National Museum of the American Indian, Dated as of November 1, 1991.

6/ Two versions of *The Heye & the Mighty* exist. One, written by Roland Force & submitted to the University of Oklahoma Press, 1995, appeared only in manuscript. After his death, editors doubled its size to 504 pages & printed it as Force, 1999.

7/ Force, 1999, all quotes.

8/ Specimen 19/2685.

PETROGLYPH:

1/ Schoolcraft. 1853: illus. 18.

ABRAMS, GEORGE H.J.

1995 Race, Culture, and Law, Notable Native Americans, edited by Sharon Malinowski, Gale Research, Inc.

ALEXANDER, CAROLINE

1994 Little Men, Outside Magazine, April issue.

BARNHART, TERRY A.

1998 Search for the Mound Builders, Ohio History, 107, Columbus.

BELMONT, F.V. DE

1952 History of Brandy in Canada, Mid-America, 34:42-63, Chicago. Translated from Historie de l'Eau-de-Vie en Canada, Collection de Memoires et de Relations sur l'Historie Ancienne du Canada, Societé Litteraire de Québec, 1840.

BERNIER, JOSEPH E.

1939 Master Mariner and Arctic Explorer, Le Droit, Montreal.

BIRD, JUNIUS

1960 See Kevin Wallace, ms. Profile of George Heye, Rare Books & Manuscripts, Box 1487, Folder 10; New York Public Library. A reduced & edited version of this appears in Wallace, 1960.

BODGE, GEORGE MADISON

1906 Soldiers in the King Philip War, privately printed, Boston.

BOUCHER, P.

1883 True and Genuine Description of New France, edited by E.L. Montizambert, Montreal.

BROWN, ALISON K.

1998 Revealing Histories: A Cross-cultural Reading of the Franklin Expedition to Canada, in Reading beyond Words: Context for Native Histories, edited by J. Brown & E. Vibert, Broadview Press, Peterborough.

2001 Catalogue of the Rymill Collection of the University of Cambridge Museum of Archaeology and Anthropology, Journal of Museum Ethnography 2001.

BURCH, WANDA

1990 Sir William Johnson's Cabinet of Curiosities, New York History, 71/3, Cooperstown.

BURNETT, E.K.

1964 Transcript of tape recording. Oral history of the Museum of the American Indian, NMAI Archives, VW:13:1-26.

CADZOW, DONALD A.

1926 Bark Records of the Bungi Midewin Society, Indian Notes and Monographs 3, Museum of the American Indian, Heye Foundation, New York.

1929 Air-cooled Adventure among the Aborigines: Franklin Car Penetrated Where Automobile Never Went Before, Franklin Automobile Company, 12 pages, Syracuse, New York.

CARPENTER, EDMUND

1942 Iroquoian Figurines, American Antiquity, 8/1:105-113. Initial survey made in 1938.

1956 The Irvine, Cornplanter and Coydon Mounds, Pennsylvania Archaeologist, 26/2.

2002 European Motifs in Protohistoric Iroquois Art, in William L. Merrill & Ives Goddard (editors), Anthropology, History, and American Indians: Essays in Honor of William Curtis Sturtevant, Smithsonian Contribution to Anthropology, 44, Washington.

CECI, LYNN

1986 Tracing Wampum's Origins: The Bead Evidence from Archaeological Sites in Western and Coastal New York, Proceedings of the 1986 The Bead Conference: Selected Papers, edited by Charles F. Hayes III, Research Records 20, Rochester Museum & Science Center, Rochester.

CHARLEVOIX, P.F.X. DE

1923 Journal of a Voyage to America, edited by L.P. Kellog, Chicago.

COREY, ALBERT B. (editor)

1921-1962 The Papers of Sir William Johnson, University of the State of New York, Albany.

CULIN, STEWART

1901 A Summer Trip among the Western Indians, Bulletin, Free Museum of Science and Art, University of Pennsylvania, 3/3, Philadelphia.

1905 Expedition Report, 1905. MS in the Anthropology Archives, Brooklyn Museum, New York.

1908 Expedition Report, 1908. MS in the Anthropology Archives, Brooklyn Museum, New York.

DAVIDSON, D.S.

1937 Snowshoes, American Philosophical Society, Memoir series, Philadelphia.

DAVIS, MARY B.

1987 Field Notes of Clarence B. Moore's Southeastern Expeditions, 1891-1918. A Microguide to the Microfilm Edition, Huntington Free Library, New York.

1987 Papers of the Hemenway Southwestern Archaeological Expedition in the Huntington Free Library: A Guide to the Microfilm Edition, Huntington Free Library, New York.

1991 The Wabanaki Collection and the William Wallace Tooker Papers in the Huntington Free Library: A Guide to the Microfilm Edition, Huntington Free Library, New York.

DEWDNEY, SELWYN

1975 The Sacred Scrolls of the Southern Ojibway, University of Toronto Press, Toronto.

DOUGLAS, FREDERIC & RENÉ D'HARNONCOURT

1941 Indian Art in America, Museum of Modern Art, New York.

DUNCAN, KATE C.

2000 1001 Curious Things: Ye Olde Curiosity Shop and Native American Art, University of Washington Press, Seattle.

DUNDAR, JOHN TELFAR

1962 History of Highland Dress, Edinburrgh & London.

DWIGHT, TIMOTHY

1810 Travels in New England & New York, 2 vols., privately printed, New Haven.

EVERARD, H.

1891 The History of Thos. Farrington's Regiment, Subsequently designated the 29th [Worcestershire] Foot, 1694-1891, Worchester Press, Worchester.

EWERS. JOHN C.

1959 Crow Indian Beadwork, Museum of the American Indian, Heye Foundation, New York.

1960 Crow Indian Medicine Bundles, Museum of the American Indian, Heye Foundation, New York.

FENTON, WILLIAM N.

1989 Return of the Eleven Wampum Belts to the Six Nations Iroquois Confederacy on Grand River, Canada, Ethnohistory, 36/4:392-410.

FIENUP-RIORDAN, ANN

1996 The Living Tradition of Yup'ik Masks, University of Washington Press, Seattle.

FISHER, CHARLES L. (editor)

2003 People, Places, and Material Things: Historical Archaeology of Albany, New York, New York State Museum, Bulletin 499, Albany.

FLICK, ALBERT C. (editor)

1939 The Papers of Sir William Johnson, University of the State of New York, Albany.

FORCE, ROLAND W.

1995 The Heye & the Mighty, unpublished manuscript.

1999 The Heye & the Mighty, Mechas Press, Honolulu.

GIBSON, SUSAN G. (editor)

1980 Burr's Hill: A 17th Century Wampanoag Burial Ground in Warren, Rhode Island, Haffenreffer Museum of Anthropology, Brown University, Providence.

GILMAN, CAROLYN & MARY JANE SCHNEIDER

1987 The Way to Independence. Memories of a Hidatsa Indian Family, 1840-1920, Publications of the Minnesota Historical Society, Museum Exhibit Series, 3, St. Paul.

GIROUARD, MARK

1984 Life in the English Country House, New Haven & London.

GRANT, SHELAGH D.

2005 Arctic Justice: On Trial for Murder, Pond Inlet, 1923, McGill-Queen's University Press, Montreal.

HALL, CHARLES F.

1879 Second Arctic Expedition, 1864-1869, edited by J.E. Nourse, Washington.

HALL, COURTNEY ROBERT

1934 A Scientist in the Early Republic: Samuel Latham Mitchell, 1764-1831, Columbia University Press, New York.

HALLOWELL, A.I.

1926 Bear Ceremonialism in the Northern Hemisphere, American Anthropologist. Vol. 28/1.

HAMELL, GEORGE R.

1979 Of Hockers, Diamonds and Hourglasses, paper presented, Iroquois Conference, 10.13-15.79, Albany.

HEYE, GEORGE G. & GEORGE H. PEPPER

1915 Exploration of a Munsee Cemetery near Montague, New Jersey, Contributions, Museum of the American Indian, Heye Foundation, 2/1, New York.

HOLM, BILL & WILLIAM REID

1975 Form and Freedom, Rice University, Houston.

JORDAN, JOHN W.

1909 Adam Hubley, Jr., Lt. Col. Comdt., 11th Penna. Regt., His Journal, Commencing at Wyoming, July 30th, 1779, Pennsylvania Magazine of History & Biography, Philadelphia.

KING, J.C.H.

1994 Native Art as Depicted by Charles Hamilton Smith, 1816-1817, American Indian Art Magazine, Spring issue.

KING, ELEANOR M. & BRYCE P. LITTLE

1986 George Byron Gordon and the Early Development of the University Museum, in S.A. Kaplan & K.J. Barsness, Raven's Journey, University Museum, Philadelphia.

KINIETZ, W.V.

1940 The Indians of the Western Great Lakes, 1615-1760. Occasional Contributions, Museum of Anthropology, University of Michigan, Ann Arbor.

KRECH, SHEPARD III (editor)

1994 Passionate Hobby: Rudolf Frederick Haffenreffer and the King Philip Museum, Haffenreffer Museum of Anthropology, Brown University, Providence.

LAFITAU, JOSEPH-FRANÇOIS

1724 Moeurs des sauvagues ameriquains. . . . , Paris.

LEACH, DOUGLAS EDWARD

1958 Flintlock and Tomahawk, Macmillan, New York.

LENDER, MARK E. & JAMES KIRBY MARTIN (editors)

1982 Citizen Soldiers: The Revolutionary Journal of Joseph Bloomfield, Newark.

LENZ, MARY JANE

2004 No Tourist Material: George Heye and His Golden Rule, American Indian Art, 29:4.

LÉVI-STRAUSS, CLAUDE

1943 The Art of the Northwest Coast at the American Museum of Natural History, Gazette des Beaux-Arts, 24.

1979 The Origin of Table Manners, Harper & Row, New York.

1985 The View From Afar, Basic Books, New York.

LORING, STEPHEN

1985 Boundary Maintenance, Mortuary Ceremonialism and Resource Control in Early Woodland: Three Cemeteries in Vermont, Archaeology of Eastern North America, 13.

LOTHROP, ELEANOR

1948 Throw Me a Bone, illustrated by John O'Hara Cosgrove II, McGraw-Hill, New York.

LOTHROP, SAMUEL K.

1957 George G. Heye Obituary, American Antiquity, 23:66-67, Menasha.

LOWIE, ROBERT H.

1959 Robert Lowie, Ethnologist: A Personal Record, University of California Press, Berkeley.

MASON, J. ALDEN

1958 George G. Heye, 1874-1957. Leaflet, Museum of the American Indian, Heye Foundation, New York.

MYER, ROY W.

1977 The Village Indians of the Upper Mississippi: The Mandans, Hidatsa, and the Arikasas, University of Nebraska Press, Lincoln.

MYERS, ROBERT M.

1984 Children of Pride: a True Story of Georgia and the Civil War. New York.

MITCHELL, SAMUEL L.

1817 American Antiquities, Letter from Samuel L. Mitchell ... New York, January 13, 1817, Port Folio, for May, 1817. Reprinted in Archaeological Americana Transactions and Collections of the American Antiquarian Society, vol. 1:313-355, 1820. Reprinted in Franklin Fenengo, 'An Early 19th century Account of Assinibone Quillwork,' The Plains Anthropologist, 3:19-22, April, 1955. See Mary Jane Schneider, Plains Indian Art, 1980.

NABOKOV, PETER

1967 Two Leggings: The Making of a Crow Warrior, Crowell, New York.

NOYAN, P.

1912 Memorandum Concerning the Present Conditions of Canada, 1720, Michigan Pioneer and Historical Collections, 34.

O'CALLAGHAN, E.B.

1849-51 Documentary History of the State of New York, Albany.

PARKER, ARTHUR C.

1913 The Code of Handsome Lake, New York State Museum Buelletin, 163, Albany.

PARKS, DOUGLAS R.

1992 Introduction, in A. Bowers, Hidatsa Social and Ceremonial; Organization, University of Nebraska Press, Lincoln.

PEPPER, GEORGE H.

1905 Memo to George Heye, Anthropology Archives, American Museum of Natural History, New York.

PEPPER, GEORGE H. & GILBERT L. WILSON

1908 An Hidatsa Shrine and the Beliefs Respecting It, Memoirs of the American Anthropological Association, 2:275-328.

PHILLIPS, RUTH B. & DALE IDIENS

1994 A Casket of Savage Curiosities, Journal of this History of Collections, 6/1, Oxford.

PRINCE, J. DYNELEY & FRANK G. SPECK

1904 Glossary of the Mohegan-Pequot Language, American Anthropologist, (N.S.), 6/1.

Proceedings of the General Court Martial at German Flats on July 29, 1776, Papers of the Third New Jersey Regiment, New York State Library, Misc. papers, Albany.

███████████, █████ & █████

    ████ ███ ████████ █████ █████████ ██ ███ █████████ █████████, ███ ████.

1910 The Antiquities of Manabi, Ecuador: Contributions to South American Archaeology, 2 vols., New York.

1929 Bibliographic Notes on the Shrinking of Human Heads in South America, Indian Notes, 6/1:56-74, New York.

SAWIN, MARTICA

1995 Surrealism in Exile and the Beginning of the New School, MIT Press, Cambridge.

SCHELLBACH, LOUIS

1928 An Historic Iroquois Warclub, Indian Notes, 5/2, Museum of the American Indian, New York.

SCHOOLCRAFT, HENRY R.

1853 History, Condition and Prospects of the Indian Tribes of the United States, vol. 3, Philadelphia.

SCHUSTER, CARL

1986 Social Symbolism in Ancient & Tribal Art, vol. 1, Rock Foundation, New York.

SCHUSTER, CARL & EDMUND CARPENTER

1996 Patterns that Connect, Harry N. Abrams, New York.

SEMPOWSKI, MARTHA & LORRAINE P. SAUNDERS

2001 Dutch Hollow and Factory Hollow, Research Records, 24/1, Rochester Museum & Science Center, Rochester.

SHEARS, BRENDA

1987 Field Notes and Maps of the Hendrick-Hodge Archaeological Expedition, 1917-1923: A Guide to the Microfilm Edition, Huntington Free Library, New York.

SHOEMAKER, INNIS HOWE (editor)

1999 Mad for Modernism: Earl Horter and His Collection, Philadelphia Museum of Art, Philadelphia.

SMITH, J.G.E.

1980 Arctic Art: Eskimo Ivory, Museum of the American Indian, New York.

SMITH, MURPHY D.

1987 A Museum: The History of the Cabinet of Curiosities of the American Philosophical Society, American Philosophical Society, Philadelphia.

SMITH, WATSON & RICHARD B. WOODBURY & NATALIE S. WOODBURY

1966 The Excavation of Hawikuh by Frederick Hodge: Report of the Hendricks-Hodge Expedition, 1917-1923, Contributions, Museum of the American Indian, no. 20, New York.

SPECK, FRANK G.

1924 Eskimo Collection from Baffin Land and Ellesmere Land, Indian Notes, 1:143-149, Museum of the American Indian, New York.

1928 Native Tribes and Dialects of Connecticut, 43rd Annual Report of the Bureau of American Ethnology, 1925-1926, Washington.

STEIN, SUSAN R.

1993 The Worlds of Thomas Jefferson at Monticello, Harry N. Abrams, New York.

STONE, WILLIAM L.

1865 Life and Times of Sir William Johnson, Bart, 2 vols., Albany.

THWAITES, R.G. (editor)

1896-1901 Jesuit Relations and Allied Documents, 1601-1792, 74 vols., Cleveland.
1904-1907 Early Western Travels, 31 vols., Cleveland.

TOOKER, ELIZABETH

1998 A Note on the Return of Eleven Wampum Belts to the Six Nations Iroquois Confederacy on Grand River, Canada, Ethnohistory, 45/2.

TREMBLAY, ALBERT

1921 Cruise of the Minnie Maud, Arctic Exchange and Publishing, Québec.

VERRILL, A. HYATT

1955 Autobiography, manuscript, NMAI Archives.

WALLACE, KEVIN

1960 A Reporter at Large: Slim-Shins' Monument, New Yorker, 36 (19.11.60:104-146).

WARDLE, H. NEWELL

1929 Wreck of the Archeological Department of the Academy of Natural Sciences of Philadelphia, Science, 70 (1805):119-121.

WEEDEN, WILLIAM B.

1884 Indian Money as a Factor in New England Civilization, Johns Hopkins University Studies in Historical and Political Science, 2nd series, nos. 8-9, Baltimore.

WIERZBOWSKI, WILLIAM

1999 Horter's Native American Collection, in Shoemaker, 1999.

WILSON, GILBERT L.

1906 Diary 3, Wilson Papers, Archives, Minnesota Historical Society, St. Paul.
1907 Diary 5, Wilson Papers, Archives, Minnesota Historical Society, St. Paul.

WOLF, CHIEF

1911 Anthropology Archives, American Museum of Natural History, New York.

SET IN SABON TYPE

PRINTED BY THAMES PRINTING COMPANY ON DULCET PAPER

DESIGNED BY JERRY KELLY